Reflections on Race
From Jim Crow to Black Power and Black Lives Matter

James Robert Ross
a white southerner

with

Joe Smith
a black southern police officer

Dedicated

To All the People of Color
Who Have Struggled with Both Courage and Grace
To Affirm Their Status as God's Children

CONTENTS

Introduction

Many of the essays here were inspired by the Civil Rights Movement and were originally published in the sixties and seventies in religious journals. Others, especially those toward the end of the book have not heretofore been published. The last three chapters were written specifically for publication in this collection of essays.

My target audience especially in the sixties was primarily white society, more specifically white churches in the South, which minimized or denied the racism and its manifestations not only in their community but in their churches. Nevertheless, some of the chapters in this book will be of interest to African-Americans, especially the introduction to my book on the debate in the black community regarding the strategy on nonviolence to effect racial justice, the chapter on the sexual roots of racism and some of my personal reflections on the current state of the African-American community.

My own reflections close with a chapter on Martin Luther King's unfulfilled dream of justice and reconciliation more than a half century after the Civil Rights movement. The founding of this republic upon the principle of the equality of all men and women with the goal of establishing a truly democratic society has been sabotaged from the founding of our nation with the infectious poison of slavery. Sadly the accomplishment of racial justice and equality has not been fully achieved by Abraham Lincoln's Emancipation Proclamation, nor by the nineteenth century's post Civil War amendments to the Constitution, nor by the Civil Rights Act of 1968. Thus we must continue our conversation on race, and to that end I offer these reflections of one old pale male.

Finally, I have asked a good friend and fellow Rotarian, Joe Smith, to respond with his perspective on race. He writes from the point of view of an African-American, who was born, educated, and worked as a law enforcement officer in he South.

Growing Up in a Racist Society

Born in 1934 in Clarksville, Tennessee, I am a child of the South, the pre-civil rights, segregationist South. My father was a postal worker, mother a traditional stay at home mom. At age three my family moved to our ancestral home in rural West Tennessee. My family's roots can be traced to my great-great-great-grandfather, James Ross, a seventeenth century Scottish immigrant, who settled in Columbia, South Carolina. His will informs us that he was the owner of at least one slave, a "negro girl by name of Pam," whom he bequeathed to his wife, Caty upon his death in 1820. His son, Daniel Ross, moved from South Carolina to Tennessee in the early nineteenth century. His will makes no mention of slaves in his will, which was written in 1841.

My parents moved with their five children to Knoxville in 1944 where I completed my public school education in racially segregated schools. Tennessee like all of the South was a thoroughly racist society. We were not only racist but also contented with our racism and with segregation as a way of life. Blacks did not complain, at least not out loud. I never saw an African-American step over the lines, some visible and others invisible, which clearly prescribed their subservient role. As long as blacks kept their place, we were content.

Most of us believed that our black neighbors were also happy with these arrangements. And since we never heard anyone complain and since we never witnessed any protest marches or sit-ins, we, like Phil Robertson, the Louisiana star of Duck Dynasty, convinced ourselves that our black neighbors were as contented with segregation and Jim Crow as we whites. As a child I never heard anyone, black or white, question this system or criticize it in any way. It was just the way things were.

In *Everything That Rises Must Converge* by Flannery O'Connor Julian's mother refuses to sit by a black person on a bus after they were integrated. Her comment illustrates the prevailing condescension of the South toward African-Americans when I was a child. She said, "I remember the old darky who was my nurse, Caroline. There was no better person in the world. I've always had a great respect for my colored friends. I'd do anything in the world for them and they'd . . ." All of us, like Phil Robertson of Duck Dynasty fame, actually believed that blacks were contented with their lot in life.

Thus an entire culture, including an economic system, had been built upon slavery, segregation, and the exploitation of African-Americans for the advantages of the dominant Anglo culture. This system seemed normal to anyone like myself who grew up in it. I never witnessed lynches or other atrocities committed against people of color. I do not remember hearing a great many racist remarks or seeing African-Americans physically or verbally abused, especially in my own family, which treated our colored servants with measured civility, even, respect. I did, however, learned to use all the common racially based proverbs such as "sweating like a nigger at election time."

On the other hand, within many households there was sometimes a kind of intimacy between black caretakers and the children often left in their care. When I was an infant, my mother brought a black nanny into our home to help with my care. Given my appreciation for the power of the unconscious and for what has been called somatic memory, I wonder what profound psychological imprint might have been made on my soul by the intimate contact of this woman's black skin with my white skin.

Every other contact up until age ten which I had with a black was filtered through the perspective of segregation and all that it entailed including the work they did for us whites. For a time we had a black maid, who stayed with us, sleeping on a cot in the attic. She did housework but, of course, never ate at our table. When it came time to pick cotton, we depended upon cheap African-American labor. At hog killing time we paid our black help with the parts of the pig for which we had no use–the tail, the feet, the head, and the intestines used to make chitlins.

I don't know whether or to what extent my parents and their decent, polite, civilized, church-going peers perceived the injustice in this economic system. Perhaps the jokes they told about how colored folk loved chitlins and watermelon was a way of rationalizing and denying the prompting of their conscience.

Not often, but once or twice, I remember playing with a black child. It seemed to me that other than the color of his skin he was not too different from myself. I don't remember wondering why it was important that he not drink at the water fountain at the county court house, and I never asked, and I certainly did not lose any sleep over it.

After we moved from rural West Tennessee to Knoxville in 1944, I had less contact with African-Americans. Nevertheless, about 1950 when I was perhaps sixteen years old my response to racial discrimination became radicalized. It happened in a bus station in Nashville, TN. I was on my way by bus from Knoxville to visit my grandmother in West Tennessee. This was the first time I had ever traveled alone for that distance, and I felt quite grown up.

During the Korean War buses and trains were the major means of public transportation, and they were always crowded. It was necessary for me to change buses in Nashville. When I got ready to board the west bound bus, there were two African-American soldiers dressed in starched khaki uniform directly in front of me in the queue.

The driver appeared and began taking tickets and boarding passengers. When he came to the two black soldiers, he simply passed them and asked for my ticket so that I could board. After all the whites were boarded and had been seated, the two soldiers and other Afro-Americans would then be boarded. They might sit in the rear, if there were seats left. Since the bus was crowded they would have to stand. That was the way it was.

I do not know why I did what I did. Nobody had ever taught me to do so. I had never heard of anyone doing so. Indeed, everything that I had seen and heard for the first sixteen years of my life led me to understand that the bus driver was doing what was right and normal and that the right and normal thing for me was to move up ahead of the blacks, hand the bus driver my ticket, get on the bus and seat myself.

Mother called me a strong-willed child. Perhaps this explains my action. I don't think that I was more socially sensitive or morally responsible than anyone else. But whatever the explanation, when the bus driver refused to board the black soldiers in front of me and asked for my ticket, I said to him, "Sir, these two men have been waiting in line in front of me."

The driver instantly flew into a rage, and with some colorful obscenities told me that if I wanted to ride the bus, I better shut up and get on the bus. I would like to tell you that I was a hero—although today I can guess that the two black soldiers were saying to themselves that this white boy better shut his mouth before we all get in trouble. But I felt completely humiliated and put in my place. Without further protest, I gave him my ticket and boarded the bus. But my eyes had been opened. I saw with utter clarity the ugly, evil face of segregation and the underlying racism which kept it in place.

After getting married at age twenty and spending three years in Kentucky starting my college education, Doris and I moved to Ponchatoula, LA, where from 1956 to 1958 I preached at a small mission church and attended classes at Southeastern Louisiana College. In the course of my pastoral visitation I was bold—my friends would say "foolhardy"—to go calling in the black community, which was a short distance from our storefront church building.

I was welcomed by one elderly black couple, Mr. and Mrs. Alfred Atkins, who consented for me to offer a Bible study in their home for them and any neighbors who might attend. I even had the hutzpa to ask them to attend my church's Wednesday night Bible study. Amazingly they had the courage to accept my invitation. Boy, was that a cold night in July in Louisiana! Wisely they never came back.

Nevertheless, Mr. and Mrs. Atkins asked for baptism, which thrilled me as a young preacher looking for souls to save. Our small church had no baptismal pool, but in the past we had been welcome to use the baptistry at a sister congregation in Amite, a few miles north. So, naturally, we took the Atkins to the Amite church to be baptized where we were unsurprisingly turned away. Thankfully the Tangipahoa River had not yet been declared off limits to blacks by the White Citizens Council.

We moved in 1958 to Atlanta where we lived until 1962 while I finished college and attended Columbia Theological Seminary. I preached at a small church in Hapeville on the south side of Atlanta, and to make extra money for a growing family I worked part time at Baker's Shoe Store on Whitehall Street, just south of Five Points. Civil rights protestors marched up and down the side walks protesting the discrimination practiced by all the shops on the street. Blacks staged a sit-in at the at Woolworth's lunch counter next door.

At the store where I worked the clerks customarily addressed blacks as "customer," not "Miss," and always seated them at the rear of the store. That changed rather quickly, however, when blacks began a boycott of stores that discriminated against them including Baker's Shoe Store where I was employed. When blacks stopped buying our shoes, we were given strict orders to let them sit wherever they liked. This flexibility on the part of the management gave me a deep appreciation for the power of the dollar to achieve what moral arguments could not.

I followed closely the progress of the civil rights movement throughout the South. On one occasion I had the privilege of meeting Dr. Martin Luther King. Never reticent to express myself I began writing about segregation. My first essay, "You Are the Man," reprinted here, condemned the racism in our churches. The *Atlanta Journal* published my letter to the editor in of support of the cause of civil rights and the sit-ins taking place in Atlanta and elsewhere in the South.

After seminary I took a position from 1962 to 1966 teaching Bible and philosophy at a small junior college in Winchester, KY. When the college integrated by allowing a local black pastor to take a few classes, it was a big deal among our supporting churches. One of the elders and his wife at my former pastorate in Georgia expressed considerable anxiety about how the presence of a middle aged black pastor on campus might lead to a romantic attachment with their daughter who was enrolled there. Thankfully neither the young coed nor the pastor ever showed much romantic interest in each other. (For my take on this fear see my essay on "The Sexual Roots of Racism.")

In 1966 I returned to Atlanta to enroll in a program of doctoral study at Emory University. The attitude on the Emory campus towards the goals of the civil rights movement was considerably more liberal than in the surrounding Georgia culture. After the assassination of Martin Luther King on April 3, 1968, I was privileged to march in the procession memorializing his life and death.

After graduate school I spent two years teaching at Alabama A&M, a predominantly black university. My responsibility to teach an introductory class in philosophy led me to explore the debate within the black community regarding the method of nonviolence used by Dr. Martin Luther King to advance the cause of racial justice for blacks. This research was published in under the title *The War Within: Violence or Nonviolence in the Black Revolution* (Sheed and Ward, 1971).

At Alabama A&M I had an opportunity to interact on a daily basis with the black faculty and student body. I observed that the black power structure represented in the university faculty and administration had strong roots in the black church. The influence of their faith was reflected in the opening of all faculty meetings with a prayer by the university's chaplain. The dominant liberal and secular culture, especially in the years following the early success of the civil rights movement, has failed to give sufficient credit to the Christian faith of the black leaders which motivated them to risk their lives for the sake of their freedom and that of their children.

Since leaving Alabama A&M in 1970 I have had much less opportunity to interact with blacks. Many of us on both sides of the racial divide hoped that we were finally on the road to justice for all without regard to color or any other identifying traits. In my last essay in this collection I will reflect on the extent to which these dreams have been realized.

You Are the Man

Originally Published in the *Word and Work* January 1969

The [1964] July ninth issue of *Firm Foundation,* a prominent publication of the Churches of Christ, carried an editorial and several articles which were critical of a call by Walter Burch for Christians to become more involved in the contemporary Negro struggle for social justice. The original article by Burch and those in reaction to it raised several important issues, one of which we propose to discuss in this essay. Most of the articles critical of Burch's view assume what the editorial itself bluntly stated, "that racial prejudice is gross in an infinitesimally small part of the body of Christ."

Personal contact with Negroes including considerable contact over the past few months as a teacher at a predominantly Negro college, and observation of public media point to a contradictory assumption, *viz.,* that practically all whites, including members of the churches of Christ, are guilty of gross racial prejudice. The disagreement between black opinion and white Christian editorials is, to say the least, disturbing. Either our black brethren are unjustly accusing us or else our hearts arc terribly hardened to sin.

Are we using identical words to mean different things? If by racial prejudice the white Christian means overtly hostile acts toward Negroes, then the editor of the *Firm Foundation* is probably correct in maintaining his innocence. Most of us have never gone out of our way to insult anyone, black or white. Only a minute proportion of our population has ever thrown a fire bomb into a Negro's home or into a black Sunday school class. Perhaps no member of the churches of Christ is guilty of that kind of prejudice.

Or we might define prejudice as the refusal of a sepulchrally white church to baptize a black penitent believer in the colorless waters of its baptistry. I can personally attest that this and like atrocities have been visited upon Negroes by churches of Christ.[1] But let us assume that even this type of discrimination is found in only a very small part of the body of Christ.

There is another definition of prejudice and racism, the definition by Otto Kerner, Chairman of the President's National Advisory Commission on Civil Disorders. He says, "I define racism as the deeply rooted system expressed in the belief that if you are white, you are superior—and it you are black, you are inferior." The "system" which the black man sees as evidence of genuine racism was for many years characterized by the insults of back seats—or no seats—on public transportation, by separate and unequal schools, by back door entrances to restaurants, by "white only" signs at golf courses, beaches, theaters, churches and schools, including churches of Christ and Christian colleges.

Those of us who did not personally pass Jim Crow laws or erect "white only" signs accepted them almost to a man without protest. To this day most of us have not publicly apologized for them. We were happy with a rigidly segregated society, and most of us complained when a "godless" Supreme Court began slightly revising it. The system granted many privileges to those of us who are white. By accepting these privileges we were brainwashed into accepting the premise on which they rested, namely that whites are superior and blacks are inferior. We, I, became prejudiced without knowing it.

I write this, not in judgment upon bigots worse than I, but in judgment upon bigots such as I. In the dark, inner recesses of my heart, places which only God knows perfectly and which are made open to us only by the grace of His convicting and quickening Spirit, I have discovered an implicit racist bent.

---

[1] My previous essay,"Growing Up in a Racist Society" describes in more detail some of my experience with racial discrimination in the Churches of Christ when I served as the minister at a small mission at Ponchatoula, LA, in the late fifties.

Superiority, however, is really found only in the humility which is revealed fully in the entrance of Jesus Christ into the world in the form of a slave (Phil 2). That superiority I do not possess. Perhaps the blacks, who have patiently washed our clothes and mopped our floors and collected our garbage and shined our shoes, are superior according to this criterion.

The question of guilt is here, as in David's confrontation with Nathan the prophet, of utmost importance. Our salvation is at stake. If there is sin, there must be confession and repentance before there can be forgiveness, newness and life.

Let us, however, be faithful to the gospel. We are not saved in the way of Baal, by self-laceration and great cries of guilt. Salvation is the gift of God in Christ Jesus. Suffering for sin was accomplished at the cross, not at inter-racial conferences or ghetto riots, although we certainly need more of the former, and we probably must endure more of the latter.

The crucial question at the moment for the white Christian is this: does he, can he or will he recognize the subtle sin which has overtaken him? Can he see that he is "the man," not communism or liberalism? The threat of God's judgment and the offer of His grace are extended to those whose conscience is pricked by the insults which have been heaped upon blacks.

Let us not deceive ourselves. Our hearts are corrupt and deceitful above all things. And the black activist may be God's Nathan—let us pray not His Nebuchadnezzar—sent to the church, His insensitive and sinful David. He points to me and you and says, "You are the man."

Salvation, healing, forgiveness and peace—between God and man and among men—depend upon confession of sin. But how can they confess who have not been convicted? And how can they be convicted who have not heard? How beautiful, then, are the black, feet which bring us the hard but healthy news of our blindness and coldness of heart.

"Therefore confess your sins to one another, and pray for one another, that you may be healed" (James 5:18).

You Can Do Something
about Race Relations

Originally published in the *Word and Work*, May 1969

The January issue of *Word and Work* carried my article on the existence and character of racism in some churches of Christ ("You Are the Man"). One concerned minister agreed with my analysis but then asked a legitimate question: "How can I as a preacher help my friends develop the kind of Christian love which will include our Negro brethren?" My remarks here are a sincere if inadequate attempt to help this Christian and others like him answer this difficult question.

We realize that we have a problem in this nation and in our churches. It is not a "Negro" problem; neither is it simply a "white" problem, nor even a "racial" problem. In its roots it is a *human problem*, the problem of sin. In this case it has produced over the centuries a terribly mutilated and divided society, and in most instances Christians have been conformed to the world rather than being transformed by the renewing of their minds in Christ Jesus. The past is not really gone. It continues to hang around our necks like a great weight threatening to pull us down into the depths of hatred and race war.

But what can we do now? I suggest three steps as at least a beginning with the hope that perhaps God will add His blessings to our feeble efforts and will have mercy on us as He did on Nineveh and spare us the horrors of increased racial divisiveness.

First, let us privately and publicly confess our sins and implore God for Christ's sake to forgive us and restore us to full fellowship with Himself and with all men, especially our black neighbors, for whom Christ died.

Second, let us begin speaking face to face and heart to heart with our black brethren in particular and with all blacks in general. Small dialogue groups have been meeting in my own home recently in order to provide blacks and whites an opportunity to express to one another their fears, misunderstandings, prejudices, hopes, and—thank God—even their love for one another. These little groups are spreading. They do nothing spectacular. But they can be organized by anyone. Eight to twelve is an ideal number, which should be fairly equally divided between the two races. They should meet in an atmosphere of cordiality, mutual trust and complete honesty. In them we whites learn how and why the blacks do not trust us. We learn why they see policemen differently than we. We learn why they still consider us arrogant and paternalistic even when we think we are only trying to help them in some way. Blacks have an opportunity to meet concerned whites, to relate to them as persons and as Christian brethren rather than as the master race.

Thus we first need to learn to speak to God and to one another about our mutual concerns. The church is the place where these things should be happening. In my own community I have found a number of interested laymen who are glad to participate in a dialogue group. It is interesting, however, that every white minister contacted, including two at the congregation I attend, declined invitations to a meeting. The white Churches of Christ in Huntsville, AL, have done almost nothing to open lines of communication with their black brethren. Whatever the reason—blindness, unconcern, prejudice or fear—it cannot possibly be justified by the Lord of the church who redeemed the church precisely as the one body in which the barriers between men are broken down (Eph. 2:11-21; Col. 3:11).

Finally, there is a third step we need to take. Just where it will lead will vary from one situation to another. Not all will have the same opportunity, talent or responsibility. But each of us can use whatever power we have to promote peace and justice in every part of our lives, as members of a church, of a business or professional organization, of a community or of society as a whole.

At this point I recommended a number of concrete proposals set forth by a group of concerned Christians who met in June, 1968, in Atlanta, Georgia. A total of thirty-five brethren said on that occasion:

> Because we love the church of Jesus Christ and want to see her fully committed to the principles of spiritual equality and racial justice for all persons, we plead for the end of discrimination in all its forms in the life of the church. To this goal the following proposals are directed. . .[2]

A Post Script—we daily receive news reports of violent clashes between militant blacks and various parts of the white community, especially school administrators and policemen. Many whites are terrified of the unrestrained passions unleashed in parts of the black community. It is, indeed, a fearful and saddening sight.

But when demoniac forces are gaining strength, that is the time above all times when those who bear the name of Jesus, that great healer of souls and exorciser of demons, should be in the thick of the battle announcing in love the gospel of peace and reconciliation. The Holy Spirit, not the prince of this world, directs our involvement in the great spiritual battles of the universe. Let us, therefore, not lose heart or be intimidated by those who hope to set men against one another and to frighten sincere Christians into silence and inaction.

---

[2] The 29 proposals are divided into six categories. Seven of these have to do with the local church; here are two sample items: No 5:. Publicize the fact that the church is open to persons of all races, if this it true. No 6: Plan all cooperative efforts in evangelism and benevolence to include Christians of all races. The complete list—about two typewritten pages in length—will be duplicated and sent to anyone who requests it. – Editor

Violence or Nonviolence in the Black Revolution

This essay introduced an edited anthology published under the same title (Sheed and Ward, 1969). The essays, mostly by black authors, focused upon the debate in the civil rights movement regarding the ethics of force and violence as a means to achieve civil rights for blacks. At the time there was a debate in the African-American community regarding the wisdom of the nonviolent tactics espoused by Martin Luther King and his followers. This debate about what tactics should be used to achieve justice and equality for blacks in America served as an introduction to the study of ethics for the students in my philosophy classes at Alabama A&M University.

The contemporary black revolution is a fact. The precise courses of action that are tactically expedient and ethically legitimate in achieving the goal of that revolution are a subject for debate even among blacks. The use of violence is one such possible course of action.

Discussions about violence are not merely academic. Blacks have recently reminded America of its long history of violence and have pointed out that any violent action by blacks is only a response to the environment of violence to which they have long been subjected.

Because of America's self-deception about the character of its own history, especially its history of relations with minority groups such as Indians and blacks, it is today disturbed and confused, even paranoid, when it hears blacks speak of violence. These essays, which focus on the question of violence and nonviolence in the American black revolution, provide one means by which white Americans can confront their history and perhaps achieve a sane perspective on the problems facing blacks and the types of action necessary to solve those problems.

16

The debate about violence continues among blacks, and an anthology on the subject serves to make a number of divergent views accessible to those who are most immediately involved—blacks themselves.

The selections in this volume reflect and raise a number of social, economic, and political questions. Although some of these questions are receiving attention in terms of study or action, the distinctly ethical side of the debate is sometimes overlooked. Calls for violence and calls for nonviolence are both calls for action. They confront men with the need to make a decision and in so doing to say something about their view of human life, its worth, and its purpose. Because our disagreements and our fears are rooted in considerable confusion, it is helpful to distinguish and clarify various aspects of the debate.

The semantic problem . . .

The meaning of the word "violence" is not immediately and universally obvious. Many of our misunderstandings about the advocacy of violence or nonviolence are rooted in the ambiguity of the word itself. "Violence" tends to have different connotations in different social and cultural contexts. If we hope to understand one another, much less agree with one another, it is imperative to pay close attention to the meaning of the word in its particular psycho-social context.

Violence may mean deliberate, direct infliction of injury to another's body or his property. This definition is applicable to crime, on the one hand, and to self-defense, on the other. The act of injuring an intruder in one's home is basically the same sort of violence as that enacted by a mugger on the street. Both are deliberate in the sense that they are carried out with a conscious intention to cause injury. They are direct in that the injury in both cases is inflicted immediately, without a third party. The one who designs and intends the violence also commits it.

The fact that self-defense and mugging are descriptively identical is already a *prima facie* indication of the more subtle nature of the ethical distinctions which need to be made. Obviously, there is a great difference in such acts when we define them by context and ultimate intent. In the one case, violence is committed in the face of an unprovoked threat of harm to oneself or one's family. In the other, it is committed with the goal of taking another's property. However, an analysis of intent may not be sufficient to make an ethical judgment, although some ethicists maintain that only the will need be considered in judging an act. For others there is the possibility that an act of mugging by one who is starving may favorably compare with an act of self-defense by one whose goods have been unjustly gained. In certain situations, it is possible to justify the mugger and to condemn the man who defends his property.

Violence also may mean deliberate but indirect infliction of injury. Most judicial punishments fall into this category. When a man is imprisoned or executed for a crime, the injury is certainly deliberate. However, it is administered indirectly through a system of courts and prison officials who are appointed to engage in legally sanctioned violence. Insofar as police use violent tactics within the guidelines established by law, they, too, are acting for the entire citizenry. War, both by established and by revolutionary regimes, is another type of deliberate but indirect violence.

From an ethical viewpoint there are numerous problems in justifying many kinds of judicial punishment and international or civil wars. The fact that capital punishment is legal does not necessarily justify it from an ethical perspective. Although men are often conditioned to consider it their duty to take up arms at the behest of their government, there are many wars which must be judged immoral. Sometimes one side may be justified, sometimes neither. The pacificist would say that neither side is ever justified.

Violence may also refer to non-deliberate, indirect infliction of injury. For example, a social or political system may develop in such a way that certain individuals or groups inevitably suffer economic, medical, or psychic injuries. Such injuries are non-deliberate only in the sense that those who benefit from the system and generally hold positions of power within it are not consciously attempting to harm anyone. From a strictly moral standpoint, however, such individuals cannot be excused from their responsibility in continuing to acquiesce in and profit from an unjust social system.

Blacks are very much aware of this third type of violence. Conversely, most whites have great difficulty in viewing violence in such terms. They assume that America is the land of the free, that all men enjoy the same opportunities, and that if people are hungry, sick, or ignorant, it is only because they have no ambition. Any suggestion that such conditions result from violence inflicted by the majority upon the minority is met with incredulity.

It is easy for whites to think of violence when it is deliberate and direct. Riots and crimes are unquestionably condemned by the dominant groups in society. Other forms of violence such as civil punishments and international wars are justified although they are not often analyzed in terms of the human misery which results from them. The third form of violence, social violence, does not exist for the socially privileged, but it is perhaps the most fundamental reality for the disinherited and dispossessed.

When men speak of violence, therefore, it is vital to understand what sort of violence is meant. We must recognize that certain groups are likely to conceive of violence in one manner while others will conceive of it quite differently. It is essential, therefore, to study the semantics of violence and to be clear about the meanings of the words we use.

The problem of presuppositions . . .

Arguments for violence usually reflect one or more of three different basic assumptions. There is a naturalistic argument based upon a supposed biological or psychological basis for aggressive impulses in humans. For example, Frantz Fanon, William H. Grier, and Price M. Cobbs, psychiatrists who are represented in this anthology,[3] presuppose that violence is rooted in the nature of man's emotional dynamics and that aggression is the natural response of an organism that has experienced extreme suppression. Fanon's argument, however, is more deeply influenced by a second presupposition, the Marxist analysis of history and the dialectic of social change. Others such as Albert Cleage and Malcolm X reflect a black nationalist ideology. The third sort of presupposition is more pragmatic and existential. Many discussions of black power have little or no concern with ideology. They are interested only in techniques to attain desired social and political goals.

Opponents of violence also use various types of arguments. They, too, use the pragmatic argument, but to arrive at a different conclusion. Martin Luther King believed that nonviolence would produce results and that blacks would attain their goals faster through peaceful action. Barbara Deming uses many of the same arguments. Usually, however, the pragmatic argument for nonviolence tends to rest on more fundamental idealistic or religious considerations. It is argued, for example, that respect for human life demands a nonviolent approach even if it does not produce immediate or totally satisfactory changes. An adequate evaluation of the different viewpoints on violence must take account of the presuppositions on the basis of which certain actions are justified. The ethical imperative must be judged in the light of the adequacy of the view of the world and of human life implicit in it.

---

[3] Franz Fanon, *The Wretched of the Earth*, trans. Constance Farrington (Grove Press, 1963); William H. Grier and Price M. Cobbs, *Black Rage* (Basic Books, 1968).

The socio-political problem . . .

A third issue is implicit in most discussions of violence. If one grants the legitimacy of violence, at least in certain contexts, as most of us actually do, there is still a question as to which situations call for a violent response. If violence is an acceptable if regrettable instrument for maintaining the status quo or for forcing desired change, precisely when is it acceptable? How does one determine the legitimacy of a given social or political order? And how does one weigh the good to be achieved by any specific violent action against the inevitable harm which accompanies it? As James Cone asks in *Political Christian Theology* (Seabury Press, 1969), when is the indirect violence of a repressive social order worse than the direct violence of a social or political rebellion? These are the really hard questions that are raised in one way or another by every essay in this book.

Those questions are not directed to one race or another. They are addressed to us all. Hopefully, an honest hearing of them will assist us in answering them as one people rather than as two. If we can answer them as one people, perhaps we can find ways to change a violent social order without more violence.

Because we are concerned with a situation which vitally affects blacks and to which they must speak, all the authors in this volume except three are black. They focus on the question of violence as a suitable response by blacks. We assume, however, that blacks are already living in a violent society and that the question of violence is directed primarily to whites who have determined the sort of society in which we all live. Blacks, of course, are not concerned only with violence. Indeed, that is the least of their concerns. They are interested in real equality, self-determination, personal integrity, and political and economic power. Violence and nonviolence are simply alternative approaches toward more ultimate goals.

Most of the authors [represented in this anthology] reject a totally nonviolent stance. Violence may be necessary as a last resort or in self-defense. There is nothing odd or extreme in such a view. What is odd is that so many Americans are surprised to find that a human being might be driven to violence after three hundred years of slavery, injustice, and dehumanization. The seriousness of the problem facing America is underscored by the fact that violence seems to be the only possible response not only for many blacks but for other groups, both revolutionary and reactionary.

Too often, threats of violence serve only to titillate or shock. If those are the only responses evoked by this anthology, it will have failed. It is intended to communicate the feelings of a minority group to which America has too long shut its ears and to clarify the basic human and ethical dilemmas which arise from attempts to make the American dream come true for all its people.

The Sexual Roots of Racism

Paper originally presented to an interracial dialogue group
in Lexington, KY.

Biological traits and racism . . .

We are inundated by sexual images and messages–in television, in advertising, in popular periodicals and the lyrics of popular music. Nevertheless, when it comes to talking about race and sex, we are as tongue tied and Victorian as our grandparents. As West (1993) remarks, "Everyone knows it is virtually impossible to talk candidly about race without talking about sex. Yet most social scientists who examine race relations do so with little or no reference to how sexual perceptions influence racial matters."

Although cultural differences such as language, art, religion, etc. may encourage racist stereotypes, racism as such refers to the negative stereotyping of one person by another based upon racial traits, i.e., superficial biological differences that identify another person as a member of a certain race. The thesis of this essay claims that the most powerful stimulus to the racist fear and hatred of blacks by whites is rooted in an imagined biological trait without a scientific basis, namely the fantasies of whites regarding the sexuality of blacks.

Fanon (1967) observes that for whites blacks have always represented "the biological danger." Fear of blacks is rooted in a perception of the dangerous "corporeality" of blacks. "To suffer from a phobia of negroes is to be afraid of the biological. For the negro is only biological. The Negroes are animals. They go about naked. And God alone knows..." (p. 165). The leap from a simple observation of the superficial traits that characterize persons of African ancestry to this kind of perception is, of course, irrational, just as any phobia is by definition irrational.

The sexual interpretation of the biological . . .

But why does dark skin–or curly hair or thick lips–cause such a fright in whites? The explanation for this near universal phobia lies in the implicit or unconscious message about sex that whites associate with these biological traits. The fear of the superficial biological traits of blacks becomes magnified exponentially precisely because it has become associated with sexual stereotypes about blacks.   West (1993) is right. "Americans are obsessed with sex and fearful of black sexuality–the fear is rooted in visceral feelings about black bodies fueled by sexual myths of black women and men."

Gunner Mrydal (1944) made a survey of whites, who were asked what things they thought that blacks most wanted in this country. He offered his subjects a list of six possible benefits and advantages and asked them to rank order them.   The responses produced the results in the following order beginning with the privilege which whites thought blacks most highly desired:

1. Intermarriage and sexual intercourse with whites
2. Social equality and etiquette
3. Desegregation of public facilities, buses, churches, etc.
4. Political enfranchisement
5. Fair treatment in the law courts
6. Economic opportunities

Amazingly the results of a survey of blacks reported by Hernton (1965) produced the same order but in reverse! Blacks themselves state that what they value most are economic opportunities. The desire for intermarriage and sex intercourse with whites was rated least desirable.

The ultimate fear of intransigent segregationists is reflected in the ominous question, "What do you think will happen once the races start mixing?" As West (1993) observes, "Interracial sex and marriage is the most perceived source of white fear of black people–just as the repeated castrations of lynched black men cries out for serious psychocultural explanation" (pp. 86-87). Hernton adds, "The thing whites fear most about blacks is that blacks have an uncontrollable urge to mate with the sisters and daughters of white men" (p. 5).

However, on the Kentucky frontier there were a few dissenting voices. In the early nineteenth century some white leaders actually proposed intermarriage of blacks and whites as the best possible way of ultimately solving the problem posed by a large group of African-Americans living in peace with the dominant white population. An influential land owner and congressman from Kentucky, Richard Mentor Johnson, had as his wife, or concubine, a slave named Julia Chinn with whom he had several children. Christina Snyder in her book *Great Crossings* (Oxford University Press, 2017) writes that, "In forging an interracial family, Chinn and Johnson opted for what was then considered the most radical means to integrate American society [by] suggesting that whites might pacify and 'civilize' people of color through interracial marriage." Some other intellectuals, "like Kentuckian Gilbert Imlay, argued that white-black unions were inevitable and, indeed, beneficial, for they would erode slavery and prejudice, helping Americans from diverse backgrounds create a more cohesive empire."

Nevertheless, such view were dismissed and overcome by a fear of the amalgamation of the races. After the shocking defeat of heavyweight boxing champion Tommy Burns by Jack Johnson, who was black, the poet Henry Lawson in 1908, summed up the collective anxiety of whites by gloomily prophesying:

It was not Burns that was beaten
    –for a nigger has smacked your face.
Take heed–I am tired of writing
    –but O my people take heed.
For the time may be near for the mating of
    the Black and the White to Breed.

According to West, whites have become trapped by their biological-sexual stereotyping in a psychological dialectic: "seductive obsession or downright disgust."   I maintain, however, that it is not either-or, but both-and, both obsession and disgust. Fanon (1967), using a psychoanalytic interpretation, shows how the black's sexuality induces in whites both seductive obsession and disgust or fear–not one or the other but both at the same time, which explains the psychic conflict generated and the consequent difficulty in processing these feelings at the conscious level because the attraction has become repressed. The ultimate expression of this anxiety is illustrated in a quotation by Fanon of a French author, Domique O. Manoni, who puts the following question in the mouth of anxiety laden whites:

> "What," they say, if you had a daughter, do you mean to say that you would marry her to a negro?" I have seen people who appeared to have no racialist bias lose all critical sense when confronted with this kind of question. The reason is that such an argument disturbs certain uneasy feelings in them, more exactly incestuous feelings, and they turn to racialism as a defense reaction (p. 164).[4]

Flannery O'Connor in *Everything That Rises Must Converge* confirms the prevalence of this neurotic fantasy when Julian in imagining how best to shock his mother has the idea for "the ultimate horror. He [would bring] home a beautiful suspiciously Negroid woman."

Fanon points out that, "the Negro is fixated at the genital level" (p. 167). When trying to reason with my white friends in the South regarding the civil rights movement, sooner or later,

---

[4] Quoted from Prospero and Caliban: *The Psychology of Colonization* (New York, Praeger, 1964), p. 111, note 1.

they expressed their fundamental fear, "Well, you know, if they integrate the schools, the next thing is that they will start socializing–and then you know what will happen!"

Fanon vividly describes the common sexualized stereotype of the black man: "He enters puberty at the age of nine and is a father at the age of ten; he is hot-blooded, and his blood is strong; he is tough. As a white man remarked to me. . .with a certain bitterness: 'You all have strong constitutions'" (p. 167).

Fanon, a psychiatrist, reports on a free association test given to about 500 whites: French, German, English, and Italian. After developing rapport with his subjects or in the midst of other associational tests, he inserted the word Negro among some twenty other words. He writes that, "Almost 60 per cent of the replies took this form: Negro brought forth biology, penis, strong, athletic, potent, boxer, Joe Louis, Jesse Owens, Senegalese troops, savage, animal, devil, sin" (p. 166).

It is not difficult to enumerate examples of how this stereotype has permeated white culture. One does not need to quote illiterate red necks, for, as Fanon points out "even serious [and widely respected] writers have made themselves its spokesmen. So Michel Cournot could write:

> The black man's sword is a sword. When he has thrust it into your wife, she has really felt something. It is a revelation. In the chasm that it has left, your little toy is lost. Pump away until the room is awash with your sweat, you might just as well just be singing. This is good-bye. . .Four Negroes with their penises exposed would fill a cathedral. They would be unable to leave the

building until their erections had subsided..." (p. 169).[5]

Fanon then asks what Cournot's sexually explicit description might stimulate in a young girl in Lyon: "Horror? Lust? Not indifference, in any case" (p. 170). In case anyone cares, Fanon cites the results of studies which indicate that, on average, Africans and Europeans have the same length penis—in the interests of scientific accuracy, 4.6244 inches—flaccid or erect, he does not say.

Implications for the white man . . .
For the white man this sexual stereotyping means projecting onto the black man his own aggressiveness. Periodic lynches and the castration of black males demonstrate in whites both an aggressiveness toward perceived black male sexual potency and an irrational and unconscious envy of this potency, however distorted the perception. Thus white males are prevented from coming to terms with the full force of their own sexual drives, especially in its aggressive expressions. All of the unacceptable expressions of the sexual instinct that the white male experiences are conveniently projected upon the black savage. Thus, the white male never comes to terms with, never integrates, an important part of himself, namely his tendency toward sexual aggressiveness.

Implications for the white woman . . .
The anxiety about black male sexuality means that the white woman becomes invested with all the attributes of goodness and worth. She becomes a goddess, a holy virgin, who

---

[5] *Martinque*: Paris, collection Metamorphoses, Gallimard, 1948, pp.13-14.

28

must not only be protected from the animal lusts of the black man but with whom even the white man cannot be fully sexual. To the extent that the white woman buys into this distorted biological stereotype she must also deny her own sexuality. She may express her fear and horror at the descriptions of black male virility, but she cannot acknowledge publicly or own her desire for such a potent partner.

Black authors, among them Hernton and Fanon, assert a near universal desire of white women for sex with black men, even a desire for rape. This is at best an unwarranted and at worst a dangerous assertion. I have serious reservations about any man, black or white, telling women, black or white, what they want. But the fact is that white women have played an important role in a genocidal culture where black men have been systematically enslaved, lynched and castrated. White women have played the role of white goddesses, which is how they participate, however passively, in the demonization of the black male.

Implications for the black man . . .

One can also ask what Cournot's description of the potency of a black man might stimulate in a young black man in Harlem or in Main Street, USA. Laughter? Pride? Not indifference, in any case. Hernton observes that just as the white is obsessed by the idea of the Negro desiring sexual relations with whites, "the black man is secretly tormented every second of his wakeful life by the presence of white women in his midst, whom he cannot or had better not touch" (p. 2). In other words the white's sexual fears of blacks puts both sexes of both races in a box. Indeed, Hernton claims that "the sexual aspect is as much a 'thorn in the side' to blacks as it is to whites" (p. 2). The taboo against black male sexual interaction with a white female invests the idea of a sexual encounter between a black man and a white woman with a fascination totally out of proportion to the possibilities for satisfaction in such an encounter.

Hernton tells the story of how he first became acutely aware of the danger of contact with a white female. While in the fourth grade he had been walking part of the way home from school with a white girl. One day his grandmother met him, took him home and beat him unmercifully, all the while reproving him: "Do you want to git yoself lynched! Messing round wit a white gurl! A little, trashy, white heifer. Do you want to git me kilt! Git all the colored folks slaughtered..." (p. 58).

For Hernton this experience invested all potential contacts with white females with both a dreadful fear and an uncontrollable fascination, which at the same time effected a devaluation of black women, the darker the more devalued.

Implications for the black woman . . .

What, then, of the impact of sexual motivated racism for the black woman? The black female has traditionally been an object for the white male to act out his most pornographic and deviant sexual impulses. As a native Tennessean and before I was old enough to remember what it meant, I remember hearing that every real man, read "white man," had to cut his chocolate cake.

On the other hand, while she became the target of white sexual aggression, abuse and rape, the black woman could never measure up in the eyes of the black male to the ideal of the beautiful white goddess, especially if she herself was blessed with rather dark skin. If she were dark, she was ipso facto ugly and undesirable to potential black suitors. The sexual stereotyping of blacks at least furnishes the black male with a source of pride. Just because he is black he is a real stud. This necessarily subjects the black female to gratuitous sexual abuse by white males on the one hand and bias and denigration by black males on the other hand.

The way forward . . .

Is it possible that the sexual stereotyping described here has changed since the civil rights movement? In 1965 Hernton answered with an emphatic, "No." "All race relations," he said, "tend to be, however subtle, sex relations" (p. 6). Even in 1989 he was sure that in spite of changes in laws regarding interracial marriage, "the unwritten taboo (`You aren't supposed to do it!') against racial `intermingling' has not changed one iota" (p. xi). He pointed out in the original edition of the book that everyone except Southerners denies that integration will lead to intermarriage. He maintained then that the denial of liberals that integration will mean intermarriage, "functions mainly to counteract the dangerous effects that such an admission would have upon the civil right movement" (p. 181).

If it is true that racism's most powerful roots lie in the sexual stereotypes outlined here, then it seems logical that racism will never be overcome without extensive intermarriage between the races, a view that I have noted above was expressed by a few far sighted citizens in the early nineteenth century. Hernton, for one, is doubtful that this will ever happen. He asserts that interracial sexual relationships, "will never be desired and valued in and by this society and culture; it will only be exploited and employed for pornographic titillation. Only a preponderance of interracial sex relationships or large numbers of them throughout the population will humanize our behavior toward such relations. This, for reasons I have asserted, will never happen" (p. xix).

Hernton wrote these words almost a half century ago. I wonder if he remained as pessimistic about interracial sexual relationships to the day of his death in 2001. Given the sinister power of racial-sexual stereotypes he may be justified in his pessimism regarding the possibility of the acceptance of interracial marriage. Racial-sexual stereotypes continue to exert power over the imagination of both races. A poll announced in April, 2011, by Public Policy Polling reported that Mississippi Republicans' preferences going into the 2012 election revealed that 46 percent of GOP voters in the state think interracial marriage should be illegal. Among blacks one sign of the hang ups they continue to hold about black-white sexual relationships is the reluctance of single black women to consider dating or marrying a white man.

On the other hand, there is some reason to hope that the old racial-sexual fears are in decline.   One indication of the public's increased openness about interracial sex is the report of the 2010 Census that people who reported their race as both black and white more than doubled from about 785,000 in 2000 to 1.8 million in 2010. *The Rotarian* (November 2017) noted that intermarriage rates have increased more than fivefold since the 1967 supreme Court Decision Loving v. Virginia, which struck down laws banning marriages across racial lines.

There are other signs that our attitudes towards interracial contact are becoming more liberal and accepting. A 2017 Pew survey found that since 2010, the number of adults saying the increasing interracial marriage rate is good for society rose 15 point, to 39 percent. Hernton apparently was too pessimistic. A google of "interracial dating" produced not one but three websites dedicated to the promotion of black-white romantic liaisons.[6] Two of my own grand-daughters have become intimate partners with black men, and each couple has given me a biracial great-grandson.

The hold of sexual stereotypes on our minds, conscious and unconscious, will be broken only when they are openly acknowledged and when we learn to talk with one another about them and their meaning for our relationships with each other. Conversation will not destroy these stereotypes, but it can make them less fearsome. If we learn neither to fear nor to be fascinated with irrational perceptions of black sexuality, then all

---

[6] www.interracialdatingcentral.com, www.interracialmatcher.com, and www.interracialpeoplemeet.com

of us–black and white, women and men–may finally learn to act like we belong to the human race and thus be open and affirming of every type of positive relationship between black and white including sexual and marital relationships.

REFERENCES

Fanon, Frantz. *Black Skin, White Masks* (ch. 6, "The Negro and Psychopathology") Grove Press, 1967

Hernton, Calvin C. *Sex and Racism in America.* New York: Doubleday Anchor Books, 1965, 1989.

Myrdal, Gunner. *An American Dilemma.* New York: Harper & Brothers, 1944.

West, Cornell. *Race Matters.* Boston: Beacon Press, 1993.

The Action of God in the Black Revolution
Originally published in *Mission* February 1971

Where is God at work in the world today? Some people believe that God is alive only in the church, perhaps even only in a part of the church—that part to which they belong. This temptation to identify one's personal religion with the totality of the power and work of God has afflicted the people of God from the time of Jeremiah to that of John the Baptist and beyond. But the fact is that God is not limited to the church nor to Israel nor to any group of people or nation, He can anoint a pagan Cyrus or Nebuchadnezzar. Or he can raise up children of Abraham from the rocks of the earth.

It is true that the church is the place where the name of Jesus is confessed and where the gospel of God's grace toward men is proclaimed, but that does not mean that the Spirit, who raised Jesus from the dead, is at work only in the church. Therefore, if we wish to find out what God is doing in the world, particularly in the revolutionary developments in American race relations, we cannot limit ourselves to the church.

Judgment upon white racism . . .

In the light of the biblical revelation of God I see the hand of God in at least four phenomena of the black revolution. First, God appears in the work of judgment upon white racism and upon various ugly forms of oppression and discrimination in our nation. Martin Luther can help us understand this phenomenon with his distinction between the proper work of God and the strange work of God. God's proper work, that which reflects his real intention and desire for humanity, is the work of grace and mercy most perfectly accomplished in Jesus Christ. But if God loves men, he hates anything which opposes that love. The opposition of God to that which opposes his love is what Luther called God's "strange work." Thus the fiery judgment of God against all unrighteousness of men is truly the work of God.

Although it appears strange or foreign to God, who is love, it is a necessary manifestation of his character when his love for us is threatened by the evil designs of certain rebellious creatures. It is in this way that we can see how much of the apparent evil in the black revolution, for example, the hatred and destruction of property in riots, is God's strange work of judgment upon a racist society.

Stewart Alsop quotes from some of the letters, which he has received from angry blacks. One of them writes:

> Blacks endured your honky degradation and lynches and bombings. Why? Why did black people wait this long before striking back? The plain fact is we just weren't ready. . . more importantly, we were afraid to die. But honkies like you are unable to realize this because in your white myopia you think that house-niggers-in-chief....can save you from extinction. Five years from now, when you're wearing your battle gear and covering the street battles between white and black, just remember that back in 1968, one black man warned you of the coming holocaust . . .[7]

This letter reflects one of many negative and destructive signs of the black revolution, but I think we will interpret these signs correctly if we realize that God is attempting to get our attention even though he has, in a manner of speaking, found it necessary to hit us over the head with a two-by-four in order to do so. The crucial question for white America is this: can it recognize the sin which has overtaken it, a sin in which practically all of us have participated, at least through quiet acquiescence to the structures of our social order? Can the white

---

[7] Stewart Alsop, "The Coming Holocaust," *Newsweek* (March 3, 1969), 92.

Christian see that he is the man, not communism or liberalism? The promise of God's grace as well as the threat of his judgment is extended to those whose conscience is pricked by the insults which America has heaped upon the black man.

Let us not deceive ourselves. Our hearts are corrupt and deceitful above all things. And the black militant may be God's Nathan—let us pray not his Nebuchadnezzar—sent to the church, his insensitive and sinful David. He points to us and says, "You are the man." Salvation, healing, forgiveness, and peace, which are God's proper work, depend upon confession of sin. But how can they confess who have not been convicted? And how can they be convicted who have not heard? How beautiful, then, are the black feet which bring us the hard but healthy news of our blindness and coldness of heart.

Encouraging signs . . .
Beyond the judgment of God upon America in the black revolution I believe that there are several positive factors at work in our midst. There are signs that some Christians are awakening to the meaning of the commandment to love one's neighbor in a black context. Admittedly there arc contrary signs, which indicate that Christianity, especially so-called fundamentalist Christianity, continues to be the most reactionary, racist force in the nation. Witness, for example, the church bulletin in my home town of Huntsville, AL, which advertises the position of the church as (1) independent, (2) fundamental, (3) premillennial, (4) patriotic, and (5) *segregational* [emphasis added].

Nevertheless, there arc encouraging signs of the reconciling work of the Holy Spirit among God's people. President Houtz of Southeastern Christian College tells about a Georgia co-ed who was scandalized a few years ago when she learned that a middle-aged gospel minister, who happened to be black, planned to enroll in one of the college's evening Bible courses. "Why Brother Houtz," she cried, "they'll be marrying before we know it!" A few years later in a Bible study class that same young woman testified that in spite of the emotional blocks still posed by her cultural background she was learning to understand and appreciate the simple humanity of her black neighbors as never before.

I have been privileged to have a small inter-racial dialogue group in my own home, one of many that have sprung up over the country. Local congregations in the South now accept members without regard to race. All of these things are signs of a new spirit in the air, a spirit of love and compassion which can only come from the God who showed his love for us by thoroughly integrating himself with us.

It is easy for such talk of love and kindness to degenerate into an unrealistic sentimentalism, which ignores the hard problems left to us by three centuries of slavery, Jim Crow, segregation and racial discrimination. Many blacks today see a need for some degree of separatism in order to unify themselves, to explore their own solutions to their problems, and to develop black leadership. Paternalistic minded whites need to keep hands off unless they are invited to perform a specific service in the black community. However, the church of Jesus Christ has within itself no sacred walls, racial or otherwise. If we must recognize certain walls for historical reasons, we must at the same time learn to close ranks among all believers both black and white. The church, in fact, has a grand opportunity to demonstrate the power of the gospel to reconcile men to God and to one another in a relationship devoid of condescension, suspicion and bitterness.

True justice . . .

Love as a minimum requires justice. Blacks have reminded us that they really don't care about our love as long as they can receive a measure of real justice. Yet our nation has a long way to go in order to realize the ideals of justice and freedom enunciated by the Declaration of Independence, the Bill of Rights, and the prophets of Israel. At this point we would do well to recall the words of the Magnificat, Mary's hymn of praise to God for his work in conceiving within her body the Son of God:

> He has shown strength with his arms, he has scattered the proud in the imagination of their hearts, he has put down the mighty from their thrones, and exalted those of low degree; he has filled the hungry with good things, and the rich he sent empty away (Luke 1:51-53).

The God of Abraham, Isaac and Jacob and the God and Father of Jesus Christ is the God of the oppressed, the orphan and the widow. He heard the cry of a slave people in Egypt and delivered them. In the law of Moses he made special provisions for the poor. When grain or fruit was harvested, part of it was to be left in the fields for the poor (Lev 19:9-10; Deut 24:19-25). Every seven years all debts were to be forgiven (Deut 15:1-6). Who can deny that the God who made such law's takes a special concern for the sharecropper, the domestic, and the poor of every color? I cannot help but rejoice at the economic and political advances of my black neighbors. And the man who opposes such advances may find himself opposing the power of God. You may choose to fight with Pharaoh. As for me. I will fight with the God of Moses.

There are today more than five hundred elected blacks in public office. Before passage of the 1965 Federal Voting Rights Act the number was seventy. Negro voter registration has jumped more than 500 percent and continues to rise. America has a long way to go in doing right by the black man, the Indian, the Puerto Rican. the Mexican wet-back, and multitudes of poor whites. But where we see signs that justice is being done, there, we may be sure, God is at work. Shall not the God of all the earth do right?

Charles Evers, whose brother Medgar Evers, was murdered in 1963 in Mississippi, is the first post-Reconstruction mayor in that deep South state. Charles tells the story of how he and Medgar as little boys were sitting on the steps of a

Mississippi county courthouse. Senator Theodore Bilbo, a segregationist and racist from the old school, came out of the courthouse and saw the boys. "Get those niggers out of here," he said. "The next thing you know they'll be running for office." Medgar then turned to his brother and remarked, "That's not a bad idea." No, that was not a bad idea. In the words of the Magnificat God has "scattered the proud and exalted those of low degree."

The reflection of God in black . . .

My final point is most fundamental and the one least understood by many Christians. We have seen how unchristian attitudes and unjust social structures have been called into question—indeed, have received the harshest judgment in recent years. Much of this we accept as the strange work of God. In a more positive vein there are a few signs of increased compassion and understanding between blacks and whites. Another hopeful sign is the fact that blacks have begun to share a measure of this country's great economic and political power. But the most important change, I believe, is a change in black consciousness. I refer to the black man's increasing conscious identification and positive affirmation of himself as *black*. This change is symbolized in the dramatic slogans of "Black Power" and "Black is beautiful."

In many of us Black Power evokes images of blacks running through the streets looting and burning. This reaction only shows how emotional we become when our traditions are threatened and how those irrational emotions block out what is really going on around us. One of the best definitions of the economic and political significance of Black Power is found in the book by that name co-authored by Stokley Carmichael and Charles V. Hamilton.[8] They write that,

> Black Power is a call for black people in this country to unite, to recognize their heritage, to build a sense of community. It is a call for black people to begin to define their own goals, to lead their own organizations and to support those organizations. It is a call to reject the racist institutions and values of this society.[9]

Black Power is not a new gospel to which any man, black or white, owes absolute allegiance. Slogans are no better than their use, and Black Power has sometimes been misused. Nevertheless, the fundamental significance of Black Power is the black man's discovery and affirmation of his integrity and manhood. Theologically Black Power is a rediscovery and self-realization of the image of God, the reflection of God in black. In effect Black Power is a rejection of the heresy that blacks are not really human, or if they are human, that they are cursed to be the slaves of whites.

"Black is beautiful" is a poetic affirmation of the truth that all men including black men and women are created in the image of God. What God has made is good—beautiful, if you

---

[8] Stokely Carmichael and Charles V. Hamilton, *Black Power* (New York: Random House Vintage Book, 1967). I do not endorse every statement made by Carmichael, particularly those advocating violent revolution based on race hatred. My edited anthology, *Violence or Nonviolence in the Black Revolution*, published by Sheed and Ward (1971), explores the ethical dimensions of the black debate on violence.

[9] Carmichael and Hamilton, p. 44.

please. Recently one of my pale-faced friends, who is a very fundamental Christian, remarked that he had never seen an attractive black woman. In other words, black to him was synonymous with ugliness, and by implication white was synonymous with beauty. This evaluation of brown skin, thick lips, and kinky hair corrupts my friend because it leads him to assume an innate. aesthetic superiority in himself. From there it is only a short step for him to an assumption of a mental or moral superiority. (There is also a kind of irony about his aesthetic judgment since he himself is quite short, baldheaded, and in every way a non-candidate for the title of Mr. America.)

Because of the political, social, and cultural dominance of whites in our country—and to some degree because of the metaphors built into our linguistic tradition—the divinity of whiteness has not only been believed by whites but it has also infected blacks, who have been subconsciously brainwashed into believing that white is beautiful and that black is ugly. Witness the black's efforts to straighten his hair and his preference for the lighter skinned members of his race. For example, in the past a Negro family with a light-skinned daughter would often discourage her from marrying a darker beau. Negro school teachers have sometimes been accused of favoring their lighter-complexioned students. The demonic effects of this pervasive atmosphere of "whiteness" is reflected in every emotionally scarred child who hates what God has made him or her.

The janitor and yard man for our apartment building in Atlanta was a Negro, whom we called Albert. Like so many other Negroes no one ever called him by his last name or even knew what it was. He was the typical southern houseboy. He kept his place, shuffled his feet, came to the back door, and moved to the side when he passed whites on the street. Perhaps many of my neighbors felt comfortable around Albert. He certainly presented no threat to many of our long cherished customs. But I have the idea that a creature made in the image of God should look like a man and act like a man, and I feel distinctly uncomfortable around anyone whose personal dignity has been reduced to a thin, obsequious smile.

Therefore, I rejoice in the affirmation of black dignity symbolized by "Black is beautiful." Such an affirmation does not automatically guarantee sainthood. However, the most virulent hatred in a black man is a very real, if distorted, sign of his essential humanity. Only a high creature can fall so low as to hate his fellows. Only a real man can sin—or not sin. Such categories are not applicable to animals. Therefore, although I do not applaud every manifestation of racial identity and race pride. I do approve and support the sense of human dignity, which is a prerequisite for contemporary manifestations of such pride.

Twenty-First Century American Racism

Between the passing of the civil rights legislation in the twentieth century and the election of our first black president, there was reason to hope that this country's pernicious race problem might finally be on the way to a positive resolution. However, several events in 2016-17 have led many to conclude that America is just as racist as it ever was under slavery or Jim Crow. These include several police shootings of blacks, the election of Donald Trump and the death of a white woman in Charlottesville, VA, who was deliberately run down by one of the white supremacists who were demonstrating there. Prominent black commentators like Ta-Hehisi Coates would have us believe that whites are unalterably racist and that the election of Donald Trump proves it. Even their liberal white friends in Washington are given little credit for their denunciations of racism and their support of his sweeping condemnation of white America.

The genuflecting by white progressives at the feet of Ta-Hehisi Coates, who rhetorically lashes them with the charge of white supremacy, has the distinct appearance of a pathological sadistic-masochistic duet. In sado-masochistic sex one partner receives pleasure from inflicting pain while the other receives pleasure from receiving pain. The same is obvious with the symbiotic relationship between Coates and his white admirers. He enjoys heaping the most odious moral condemnation imaginable upon those who gleefully submit to it with a feeling of moral superiority because they are among the enlightened elite who have the courage to approve such a sweeping moral judgment.

I grew up among racist whites. My own parents opposed the civil rights movement and thought that Martin Luther King was a pinko, a dupe of the Communists. Today I have myself more opportunity for close interpersonal contact with blacks than most other whites. I belong to a Rotary Club, which is 85% black. Two of my grand daughters have black partners, and I am privileged to help several black clients in my counseling practice. Nevertheless, I live and move primarily among whites in my family, church and casual social relationships. These people by and large would be classified by Coates as the white, conservative and racist demographic which put Trump in office. I, therefore, have some knowledge of their views on race, especially since they speak rather openly in my presence about their feelings on the subject.

The term "racism" is too often used without a clear definition of its meaning. The word "race" itself is an artificial and divisive word that has no basis in empirical reality. But beyond the question of a unique innate prejudice of whites towards blacks, it seems indisputable that there is such a thing as group bias. People in general are more trusting of and more likely to have friends among those who are most like themselves culturally, religiously and ethnically. If this group bias is the same thing as racism, then all of us are racists, both whites and blacks. Group bias is a normal, universal trait of *homo sapiens*—and other animals for that matter. All children tend to be more reticent and less trusting of others who are different from themselves. Adults can become conscious of this normal reaction and can deliberately thwart it by choosing to move towards rather than away from the other, but that does not change the fact of the inherent default response to more away from rather than towards the other.

There is, however, something more at work in race relations especially in our country than natural group bias. We have a history of classifying one color of people, blacks from Africa, as at best created by God for slavery or at worst created as subhuman creatures. We fought a horrendous Civil War over this pernicious lie. After that war, it took us one hundred years to finally enact into law the rights of all black people that we said we believed when we asserted our independence from Great Britain in the eighteenth century.

This history is part of our national psyche, our national DNA. As such we are especially susceptible to another kind of bias that deserves the word "racism." This is the racism that believes and will attempt to enact if possible the white philosophy of pre-civil rights days: "If you are white, you are right; if you are black stay back." The real question is not about normal and universal group bias but to what extent this kind of racism still exists, and is it more prevalent than ever? The following observations do not constitute a final answer to this question. But I offer them as food for thought by one who has for over a half century struggled with it.

There are different levels and modes of racism, and I suggest that we ought to discriminate between rather than lumping them all under the same label. First, there are true believers in white supremacy, the neo-Nazis and the skin heads. They are quite vocal, and on occasion they get considerable attention in the press. There is no firm evidence regarding their numerical strength, but it is generally agreed that they represent a rather small group, less than one percent of the population. This is the extent of the most explicit and overt racism in our country.

There is, however, another group that I consider racist in the sense that they really believe in white supremacy even at an unconscious level. I call this group closet racists. In polite company they do not act or speak in a way to reveal their true feelings, but in a setting where they do not believe they will be judged, they don't mind telling a racist joke or remaking about how lazy or stupid blacks are. It is impossible to determine how large this group is. I do sometimes hear a remark that seems to reveal a closet racist. But even though I move in rather conservative circles where it is thought that racist sentiments are more acceptable, these are rather isolated events. Thus I see few signs of this sort of closet racism although it may be more easily detected by blacks than by myself.

There are, I suggest, different ways that such closet racism can be expressed. I want to differentiate among at least four different groups who have this kind of racist bias and the way that it is expressed depending upon their political philosophy and their ability to be self aware.

First, there is the political conservative who is not very much aware of his own normal racial bias. He reacts negatively to any suggestion that racism is still a problem or that blacks still endure any form of discrimination. He has trouble seeing how his own behavior often reflects a subtle bias against blacks.

Second, there is the political conservative who is aware of his racial bias and can understand that blacks still experience many subtle forms of discrimination in spite of the laws that make it illegal. He is less likely to react defensively when blacks report being the victims of discrimination and is more open to making changes, for example, in our discriminatory criminal justice system.

Third, there is the political liberal, who is not very much aware of his own racial bias. He labels his politically conservative opponents as "racist," but he responds with confusion and disbelief if anyone suggests that perhaps he and his fellow liberals have hidden prejudices that can be discerned by blacks. This person tends to see himself as without bias and is prone to take a self righteous attitude towards those who do not agree with his progressive social and political views.

Fourth, there is the white political liberal who understands the universal nature of racial bias. He is the person on the left most willing to make common cause across the political aisle with his conservative colleagues and will be less likely to use the racist epithet for his personal political gain. He is also humble enough to be on guard against his own bias

There is one other aspect of human psychology that impacts the way we see each other. The human mind inevitably sorts through a multitude of experiences by an unconscious process of generalization. If I take a certain route to work each day and almost always find it crowded with traffic, I will automatically expect to find that route in that state of congestion every time I travel it at that time. If I meet someone who is especially personable and charming and if that person continues to reflect that same personality in subsequent encounters, I will come to expect that behavior in the future.

In a similar manner when a policeman finds that most of the time when he responds to a report of a crime, that the perpetrator is black, he will come to believe that blacks are more likely to commit crimes than whites. According to statistics released by the Department of Justice during the 2012/2013 period, blacks committed an average of 560,600 violent crimes against whites, whereas whites committed only 99,403 such crimes against blacks. This means blacks were the attackers in 84.9 percent of the violent crimes involving blacks and whites. If these statistics are accurate, it is inevitable that police will make cognitive generalizations about the criminality among blacks. Even if the police do not pursue a policy of overt racial profiling, the will have a tendency to be more suspicious of blacks than of whites.

In a similar manner if a young black man has multiple encounters with whites that are demeaning or insulting, he will also conclude that this is what he should expect from all of whites. The way his brain works will move him to make that conclusion. That does not mean that the policeman or the young black male should mindlessly follow the generalized conclusions to which their experiences tend to lead them. Hopefully they can learn to acknowledge what is happening and manage this tendency toward generalization from past experience in order to prevent acting in a discriminatory manner in the future.

Although a certain route usually has more traffic than other routes, it is entirely possible that it might on some days or times have less traffic than others. Although many blacks may have committed crimes, it is obviously true that most blacks are law abiding. And although many whites discriminate against blacks or act rudely towards them, there are also whites who do not always act this way. We must learn that there are always exceptions to the rule especially when it comes to human behavior.

In conclusion with the exception of the overtly white supremacists it does not seem helpful to blame all racial slights on evil motives. If group bias is innate, then blacks are also susceptible to its influence. It is one thing for a black to politely correct a slight or a subtle form of discrimination. It is another to demonize all whites, which in some sense is the other side of white supremacy. The black person's paranoia is understandable, but when it is not controlled and leads to hostile reactions to every perceived slight, the result is increased fear, suspicion and resentment.

The Christian view of human depravity can help us understand that the universal nature of sin is reflected in many ways in all ethnic groups. This is one measure of equality that is undisputed: our shared, innate sinfulness. Historically many different peoples have been enslaved and oppressed at one time or another. Most of the African that were sold in America were originally captured and enslaved by other Africans.

Be that as it may, we cannot ignore the fact that America's history of the enslavement and subsequent discrimination of Africans has had uniquely socially disruptive consequences for the realization of our stated ideal of *e pluribus unum*, consequences with which we will struggle for a long time, thereby confirming the Biblical principle that, "The Lord God...will by no means clear the guilty; visiting the iniquity of the fathers upon the children, and upon the children's children, unto the third and to the fourth generation" (Ex 34:7).

A Dream Unfulfilled

In 1963 Dr. Martin Luther King, Jr. dreamed "that one day this nation will rise up, live out the true meaning of its creed: 'We hold these truths to be self-evident, that all men are created equal.'" We must acknowledge that to date that dream remains to a great extent unfulfilled.

The genesis of King's unfulfilled dream lies in the failure of Reconstruction following the Civil War. The War and Lincoln's Emancipation Proclamation abolished slavery, but it did nothing to change the racially biased social mores and white supremacist culture of consciousness upon which it was based. Nevertheless, abolitionist Henry Ward Beecher in his sermon of October 22, 1865, proclaimed that, "Now things are changed." History gave the lie to his words with one exception: slavery was gone forever. Otherwise not much had really changed. The racist presuppositions of slave owners and, indeed, most whites including northerners, remained essentially unchanged.

Reconstruction and the flickering lamp of genuine, meaningful freedom including suffrage was soon snuffed out by the imposition of Jim Crow throughout the South. Andrew Johnson generally takes the blame for the failure of Reconstruction. One popular narrative believes that a different outcome would have ensued had not Lincoln been assassinated. His compassion for the Negro along with his political acumen might have fulfilled the dream of real racial equality.

Nevertheless, Howard Means, who, on the one hand blames Johnson for the failure of Reconstruction, admits that, "Johnson couldn't take his [Lincoln's] place. *No one could*" [emphasis added].[10] If no one could have taken Lincoln's place,

---

[10] *The Avenger Takes His Place: Andrew Johnson and the 45 Days That Changed the Nation.* New York: Harcourt, 2006.

then it was almost a foregone conclusion that the goal of real racial equality in the South was doomed to fail. It would remain the task, not of a white leader, but of Martin Luther King, Jr. to initiate the painful and difficult process of changing the nation's consciousness regarding the racist culture that found expression in Jim Crow post-Reconstruction.

In spite of King's success in arousing the nations conscience, More than a half century later his dream, as well as that of the nineteenth century abolitionists, has only partially come true. Indeed, in many ways the condition of many blacks, excluding a small middle class, is worse off economically today than it was before the Civil Rights Movement and the War on Poverty. The explanation for this state of affairs by the progressive left is the perpetuation of slavery's systemic and structural racism.

Admittedly there is some validity to this understanding of the current plight of so many African-Americans. Lincoln in his second inaugural address tied the suffering of the nation, both North and South, to the original sin of slavery. With an astute theological insight he said that,

> if God wills that [the carnage of the Civil War] continue until all the wealth piled by the bondsman's two hundred and fifty years of unrequited toil shall be sunk, and until every drop of blood drawn with the lash shall be paid by another drawn with the sword, as was said three thousand years ago, so still it must be said "the judgments of the Lord are true and righteous altogether."

The struggle for justice and the evil consequences of slavery did not end with the Civil War. The fact that it continues to this day verifies that the sins of the fathers are visited upon the third and fourth generation and beyond (Ex 20:5).

There is, however, a trap in simply blaming slavery or other, modern structural forms of racism for the problems of the black community. Yes, racism as a personal bias still persists, but it is dangerous to assume the victim's mantel or make that one's primary identity. A victim is one who is powerless to prevent the harm inflicted upon him. By definition a victim is powerless. One can only be raped if she is powerless to flee or to overcome her attacker. I can only be mugged if the robber has a gun and I have no means of escape. When anyone, white or black, focuses solely upon the obstacles in his path to success, that focus inevitably saps him of the energy and motivation to consider and exploit whatever options might be available to overcome those obstacles.

In my professional counseling with couples I hear each partner complain about the failings of the other. The other partner is, of course, always at fault in some way or other. There is no perfect spouse. My own wife is not perfect, but I cannot change her. To the extent that I focus upon her faults, I am powerless to improve our relationship. But if I am willing to consider how I might change myself and how I might make better responses to her negative behavior, then I regain some power to improve our relationship. A focus upon either my neighbor's irrational prejudice or that of his ancestors, who enslaved my grandparents, functions to confirm my identity as a victim and becomes a hindrance in the achievement of my personal goals.

Since the victories achieved by the Civil Rights Movement in the twentieth century, legally enforced segregation is a relic of a by-gone era. Nevertheless and in spite of the election of an African-American President, racism remains alive and well in the United States. Indeed, I expect it to remain as long as we can make distinctions in the color of each other's skin or until there is a dissolution of the cultural barriers to intermarriage between blacks and whites.

Racism remains a serious social problem, but since the major victories achieved by the Civil Rights Movement, it seems to me that some blacks have unwittingly supported racism in two ways. First, when blacks suspect all whites of hostile intentions and act toward them with coldness or contempt, even when no slight was intended and no injustice committed, they discourage whites of good will. The paranoia is understandable but, nevertheless, unhelpful.

Second, to the extent that blacks wait for whites to save them and to the extent that they play on white guilt to manipulate whites to rescue them, they perpetuate their self identity as helpless victims, who need a savior, usually the white master, the great white father in Washington, D.C.

An essay, "Mental Health and Black Adolescents" *(Family Therapy Magazine,* September 2017) by Ashley Hicks White, who is herself black, illustrates what I mean by playing on white guilt. She mentions several important stressors on young black people including their cultural history of slavery, discrimination, low income, racism, and oppression . However, although she is a professional marriage and family therapist, she fails to mention the stressors implicit in the marital and family chaos that characterizes many families, black and white.

It is beyond incredible that a person who understands family systems and their impact on children could believe that the problems of the black family are not worth mentioning when addressing the needs of black adolescents. Nevertheless, Dr. White seems to believe that slavery, racism and oppression are the only problems confronting black children without offering a single solution to the way whites have victimized blacks except in the implied hope for whites to become less racist and to undo the effects of slavery and Jim Crow for their victims. Her intended audience is white society in whom she hopes to activate their guilt for the sins of their forefathers and for the racism that still exists to whatever degree among whites.

Lest there be any misunderstanding about my position on the issue of white guilt, I refer to my essay above, "You Are the Man." America's only comparable sin is the genocidal treatment of native Americans. My point is not to deny the reality of racism and discrimination but that playing on white guilt is not going to solve the problems of the black family or be of much help to alleviate the stress experienced by black adolescents. Shelby Steele put it this way, "Blacks cannot be repaid for the injustice done to the race, but we can be corrupted by society's guilt gestures of repayment."

Yes, we whites must become more self aware, a difficult but a necessary task in confronting our racial bias. A co-ed in my campus ministry fellowship who grew up in a small Illinois town in the 1960's relayed a story of our how she became more aware of her unconscious bias. She said that she was horrified about what she read and saw on television about the discrimination and violence against blacks in the South. But while working as a clerk in a shop in her small town, a black woman came to her cash register to pay for some merchandise. When she had to return change to the customer for the purchase, she suddenly became aware of a hesitancy to allow her white hand to touch the black hand into which she mst place the change for the transaction. I suspect that multitudes of whites, who like this co-ed, have had little personal contact with blacks may require some such moment of enlightenment in order to acknowledge their racial bias.

Nevertheless, whites, many of whom are in a position similar to the young lady described above, should not respond to black demands merely out of a sense of guilt. Politicians must stop pandering to blacks to get their votes. They must stop letting blacks manipulate them, and blacks must stop letting politicians manipulate them. We must expect the same level of responsibility from everyone: students, workers, athletes and public officials without regard to the color of their skin.

Some black leaders continue to talk in 2018 about the need to continue the struggle of the civil rights movement. Yes, racism is alive and well. But the civil rights movement long ago achieved its major goal of removing state sanctions to discrimination. Today one would have to search long and hard to find a place where blacks cannot vote or where they cannot use public transportation or where they are denied a civil right that can be enforced by law.

Obviously not all discrimination has been eradicated. Nevertheless, more laws making discrimination illegal are unlikely to make much difference. The African-American community has problems beyond a lack of civil rights or of police harassment. These include chaotic family systems, drug abuse, and a high crime rate. Whites of good will can support efforts to solve these problems, but the initiative must be taken by blacks themselves.

Affirmative action in education and the workplace once served a useful purpose in helping America achieve a more just society. However, if it continues to be intensively and widely implemented, there is a danger of at least two unintended negative consequences. First, it may promote a perception by whites that blacks do not deserve some of the recognition or rewards they receive. A second potential, unintended consequence is the development of a sense of entitlement among blacks that they deserve preferential treatment.

My essays in the first part of this book will confirm that in my reflections on race I have for many years refrained from telling blacks how to achieve the justice they deserve. However, after observing racial discrimination for four score years and after exhorting and rebuking my fellow whites for our racism in several published essays, perhaps I have earned the right even as an old, pale male to offer some counsel to my black friends.

At this stage in the history of race relations in America the civil rights movement has just about accomplished everything that it set out to accomplish, i.e., to remove the legal barriers to the black's full participation in America's civil and political life. It did not intend to and cannot make whites like blacks or give up their racist prejudice. The victories of the civil rights movement do not guarantee anyone success, only the opportunity to participate in the game. Sonya Carson's advice to her sons, Ben and Curtis, is worth quoting here:

Remember this as you go through life. The person who has the most to do with what happens to you is *you*! *You* make the choices; *you* decide whether you're going to give up or ante up when the going gets tough. Ultimately, it's *you* who decides whether you will be a success or not.[11]

Ms. Carson, a single, black mother, in spite of unimaginable disadvantages taught her children never to think of themselves as victims. The stance of a victim is one of powerlessness. If you are powerless, all you can do is hope that someone, most likely a white liberal, will come along to save you.

The black power movement had it right when it preached that blacks should not wait on whites to love them or treat them well. Yes, if your rights are threatened, fight for them, but run for your life from every white liberal who pities you as an inferior and wants to save you in order to assuage his guilt for the discrimination you and your ancestors endured.

Although racism will likely never be eliminated, the best way to minimize it is not to demonize whites, whose racist attitudes slip through the defenses they have learned to erect in order to appear part of a liberated, nonracist society. I can illustrate with the following story.

After our 1916 Rotary District Conference, the members of my Rotary club discussed an incident that occurred at the Convention. Conferees were gathering for a meeting when a white member of the staff of the company that arranged the Conference said to a black Rotarian, who was entering the conference, "You do realize that this is a Rotary meeting?"

---

[11] *Gifted Hands: The Ben Carson Story* (Zondervan, 2011), p. 8. I wish that half the energy expended to prevent the abuse of police power in dealing with young black men were used in making sure all boys of whatever color understood Ms. Carson's counsel.

Everyone present agreed that the best response to this insensitive comment was either to ask the company to fire the employee who made the comment or refuse to do business again with the company that hired her. I wondered, however, if this kind of punishing response, although it might be justified, would be the most effective way to advance race relations.

No question, the lady's comment to a black Rotarian deserves condemnation. I doubt, however, that she is a proud racist like those described above. Today, except for skin heads and the KKK, most folks try to keep their racism under cover in polite company. Is it possible that as naive as this lady appeared, nevertheless, she really believes that racism is wrong. Upon realizing that the black person she questioned was a Rotarian, might she have been embarrassed by her comment? Might she have learned an important lesson simply by the appearance of a black person at a Rotary meeting?

Finally, I wondered what might have been her probable reaction to a punishment with dire financial ramifications, as members of my club recommended? Yes, in the future she might be more careful in her speech around blacks in public places. But what about her attitude toward blacks? Is it possible that her implicit racial bias and stereotype, although driven underground, might become more bitter and entrenched?

One final question comes to mind. What would Dr. Martin Luther King do? Given his and his cohorts' success in advancing race relations in a hostile and much more overtly racist culture than our own, might blacks today do well to follow his example? I suggest that to publicly humiliate or punish every microaggression will do more to hinder than promote good race relations. King and his allies understood that whatever my white cultural misconceptions and biases, if you treat me like an enemy, I will likely respond in kind.

Although we have abolished many of the legal, systemic and structural foundations of racial oppression, prejudice and bias are still very real. Yet, in many ways the economic and social conditions of blacks continue to deteriorate, and the question is "why." Jason Riley writing in the *Wall Street Journal* (August 30, 2017) suggests a more convincing answer than a simplistic answer of "slavery" or "systemic racism." His critique of the progressive narrative which posits today's racial inequality as mainly a legacy of the country's slave past examines the actual state of African-Americans during Jim Crow compared to that of the post civil rights eras. He writes:

> One problem with these assumptions about slavery's effects on black outcomes today is that they are undermined by what blacks were able to accomplish in the first hundred years after their emancipation, when white racism was rampant and legal and blacks had bigger concerns than Robert E. Lee's likeness in a public park. . . Today, slavery is still being blamed for everything from black broken families to high crime rates in black neighborhoods to racial gaps in education, employment and income. Yet outcomes in all of those areas improved markedly in the immediate aftermath of slavery and continued to improve for decades.

> Between 1890 and 1940, for example, black marriage rates in the U.S. were higher than white marriage rates. In the 1940s and '50s, black labor-participation rates exceeded those of whites; black incomes grew much faster than white incomes; and the black poverty rate fell by 40 percentage points. Between 1940 and 1970—that is, during Jim Crow and prior to the era of affirmative action—the number of blacks in middle-class professions quadrupled. In other words, racial gaps were narrowing. Steady progress was being made. Blacks today hear plenty about what they can't achieve due to the

legacy of slavery and not enough about what they did in fact achieve notwithstanding hundreds of years in bondage followed by decades of legal segregation.

In the post-'60s era, these positive trends would slow, stall, or in some cases even reverse course. The homicide rate for black men fell by 18% in the 1940s and by another 22% in the 1950s. But in the 1960s all of those gains would vanish as the homicide rate for black males rose by nearly 90%. Are today's black violent-crime rates a legacy of slavery and Jim Crow or of something else?

Given the empirical data regarding the progress of blacks before the Civil Rights Movement and the regression of so many since then, we ought to be open to other answers besides slavery for the lack of economic and social progress by so much of the African-American community. One answer that suggests itself, unless one is enamored of the myth that marriage is an obsolete relic of an oppressive patriarchy, is the breakdown of an intact family with children born into, nurtured and socialized by their two biological parents. We do not have to look only at the black community to see the social consequences of divorce, cohabitation without marriage, and single motherhood. The evidence clearly demonstrates that these social arrangements are bad for children—bad emotionally, socially, legally, academically, and economically. The color of the child's skin does not matter. Other things being equal single parenthood is on the whole a disaster for children.

King believed that, "The whirlwinds of revolt will continue to shake the foundations of our nation until the bright days of justice emerge." Sadly subsequent events appear to have undermined his optimism. Instead of a more just society, we have an increase in economic disparity and, some might say, an increase in racial mistrust and animosity.

The question is what form revolt must take today in order to reverse the losses experienced by the large African-American underclass. What must happen for King's dream to be fulfilled? I do not claim to have the definitive answer to that question. However, it has been clearly demonstrated that the breakdown of the intact, two parent family can explain a lot of the distress experienced by both blacks and whites. Since that is undeniably true, it follows that the solution must in some way address the family's problems.

It remains a puzzle why African-American families began to break down precisely when the shackles of Jim Crow were being thrown off. One common explanation is the lack of employment opportunities for black men, although it might be argued that the lack of employment is an effect of the break down of the family instead of the cause of the breakdown.

I suggest two other possible social dynamics that might explain the disintegration of black families and the resultant lack of economic and social progress of many African-Americans. The first is the 60's sexual revolution and the promotion and tolerance of an individualistic and hedonistic sexual ethic by the elitist left. Many of these elite themselves choose to live by the old, traditional morals. Having children before marriage or without being married is reserved primarily today for the lower middle class, white and black, not the upper class elite.

Although this is a fact, not an opinion, we recently witnessed a bizarre outcry against an op-ed by Amy Wax, a professor at the University of Pennsylvania Law School, in the *Philadelphia Inquirer* calling for a revival of the "cultural script" that prevailed in the 1950s and continues today among affluent Americans: "Get married before you have children and strive to stay married for their sake. Get the education you need for gainful employment, work hard, and avoid idleness. . . Eschew substance abuse and crime." The dean of the University of Pennsylvania law school has described these words as "'divisive, even noxious." Half of the Ms. Wax's law-faculty colleagues signed an open letter denouncing her and calling on students to report any 'bias or stereotype' they encounter in her classroom. Student and alumni petitions poured forth accusing Ms. Wax of white supremacy, misogyny and homophobia and demanding that she be banned from teaching first-year law classes.[12] This reaction is, of course, atrociously hypocritical because the critics themselves live by and teach their children to live by the very standards they describe as indicative of white supremacy.

But whether black or white, the children raised outside of a two parent home where they are taught to get an education, work hard, and stay away from drugs are more likely to fail academically, use drugs, go to prison and bequeath their destructive lifestyle to their children. The so-called bourgeois 50's cultural norms are not the prerogative of any color or social class.

The second possible cause for the curious discrepancy between the ability of blacks to improve their condition during Jim Crow compared to the lack of progress post Civil Rights is also directly related to the breakdown of the intact, two parent home. The increase in welfare, especially for mothers of dependent children, has tended to make the presence of a responsible male provider irrelevant. In addition there is the danger of the development of a dependency that saps one's motivation and sense of personal power. As a therapist I have become aware of the damage inflicted inadvertently by parent or spouse who wants to "help" a child or spouse, who is struggling with alcoholism or drug addiction. If the family's "help" means the addict does not have to experience the consequences of his irresponsible drug or alcohol us, there is a corresponding reduction his motivation for sobriety. Recovery from addiction seldom occurs as long as the addict does not experience the consequences of his behavior.

---

[12] Wall Street Journal, 09/17/2017.

There is clearly a place for helping our neighbor in economic distress. There is also a need to avoid confirming him as a needy, incompetent child. It is not love but ignorance or self centeredness which would make an adult into a dependent child, however much it might appeal to one's sense of self importance and power to do so.

For the sake of the argument, let us ignore the evidence regarding the breakup of the family and assume that slavery or white prejudice explains the injustice and distress of today's African-Americans. If their ancestors' condition or society's discrimination is responsible today for the troubles of the black community and if their white neighbors remain infected with racial prejudice, blacks still face the question of how to respond to the unjust situation in which they find themselves. If we assume that discrimination is still rampant, blacks must themselves answer the question how they will make their life choices and what decisions they will make that have the best chance of helping them achieve their personal goals in the face of this injustice.

Surely one of those decisions must be to take whatever action is appropriate, including political action, to remove whatever obstacles lie in the way of progress. It must also include using whatever personal resources one possesses in order to achieve success in spite of those obstacles. No matter what one's past misfortunes or what injustice one's ancestors endured or what difficult conditions under which one presently lives, none of this can help a person achieve his dreams for the future except perhaps by making him a stronger, more resilient person.

None of us can change the past. None of us can change how other people look at us. This does not mean that we should accept or endure a condition over which we have some power to make a change for the better. If a change in the law or a change in my company's policies, or a move to another situation would help me, then I should do what I am able to do to effect those changes. Nevertheless, the more anyone obsesses about the past, the more they become stuck there. Victims by definition are powerless.

Is racism still alive in the twenty-first century. Yes. Do we all, blacks and whites, need to pay attention to it? Yes. Can we pay *too much attention* to it? Again, the answer is "yes," according to Dr. Alexander Jefferson, (Lt. Col. Ret., U.S. Air force), one of the renowned Tuskeegee airmen, who was shot down in 1944 and spent nine months as a prisoner of war in Nazi camps. Based on his ninety years of experience dealing with racism, he writes, "Our young people need to move beyond racism, just as we were forced to do when we were determined to fly."[13]

How does one who encounters racism "move beyond racism?" I suggests the Serenity Prayer for those who confront racial bias as well as anyone else who is confronted in life by disappointment, injustice or pain of any sort:

God, grant me the serenity to accept the things I cannot change,
the courage to change the things I can,
and the wisdom to know the difference.

Finally, I recommend to my white family and friends that they develop the practice of self examination not only because of our tendency towards group and racial bias but because it is a very necessary and wholesome spiritual exercise. We need to be aware of the fact that we are inclined to generalize our experiences in ways that are on the one hand helpful, but on the other hand, dangerous. We also ought to learn to acknowledge the pernicious, deep rooted effects of sin in our lives. The

---

[13] *Red Tail Captured, Red Tail Free: Memoirs of a Tuskegee Airman and Pow* (New Your: Fordham University press, 2017), p. 134.

purpose is not to despair but to confess our sins and repent in order that we may be forgiven. There is hope in the Good News of God's redeeming, reconciling grace in Christ.

The most intractable roots of our failure to realize King's dream of racial reconciliation and equality can be traced to our founding, to slavery and its tragic enshrinement in our Constitution.[14] This ultimately led to a division not only between free whites and black slaves but to a division between the North and the South. Abraham Lincoln referred to our founding when he attempted to call attention to, "The mystic chords of memory, stretching from every battlefield and patriot grave to every living heart and hearthstone all over this broad land."

Yet, one wonders what "mystic chords of memory" exist that could be shared by the sons of slaves with those who are the sons of slave owners? Given the difference in these memories, how could we possibly "form a more perfect union," the Civil War and the Emancipation notwithstanding? These questions, I believe, can only be answered by the God who, "from one man made all the nation" (Acts 17:26).

Remember that at one time you whites by birth, remember that you were at one time without Christ, being aliens from the commonwealth of Israel, and strangers to the covenants of promise, having no hope and without God in the world. But now in Christ Jesus you who once were far off have been brought near by the blood of Christ. For he is our peace; in his flesh he has made both groups—whites and blacks–into one and has broken down the dividing wall, that is, the

---

[14] The Constitution of 1787 included several provisions that explicity recognized and protected slavery (Art I, Sec 2 & 9; Art IV, Sec 2).

hostility between us, that he might create in himself one new humanity in place of the two, thus making peace, and might reconcile both to God in one body through the cross, thus putting to death all hostility through it. So he came and proclaimed peace to you who were far off and peace to those who were near; for through him both of us have access in one Spirit to the Father.
– adapted from Ephesians 2:11-18

Changes in Race Relations: Not All Good

At the recording of a podcast to publicize *Receptions on Race*, my black friend, Joe Smith, asked if I had experienced any changes in race relations today, 2019, compared with the Civil Rights Movement in the sixties. My answer noted the obvious positive changes. Today I would never be cursed by a bus driver because I suggested that blacks should be allowed to board and sit wherever they wished. Neither would a black be turned away from a voting booth or threatened with bodily harm or lynching if they attempted to vote. Today it is not only possible to imagine a black president, we have actually seen one. For these changes I am grateful.

I have seen some changes, however, that do not encourage me. Three stories, two from the entertainment media and one from my granddaughter, will illustrate these changes. The first story contrasts a scene in the TV series *In the Heat of the Night*, which first aired in the late 1980's, with the recent controversies surrounding Confederate monuments and other landmarks named after famous slave-holding Americans including most of our founding fathers.

In one of the episodes (season 3, episode 19) Althea Tibbs, played by the black actress Anne-Marie Johnson, gives a tour of Sparta to Regina, a black friend from out of town. Althea points out the county courthouse with its distinctive bell tower built in the nineteenth century. When they pass a large statue, Althea explains, "Sparta's own Civil War general."

Regina replies, "Confederate, of course."

Althea repeats, "Of course." They both laugh.

Two successful black women, one a teacher in the local integrated high school in Mississippi and married to the town's chief of detectives, find it amusing that a monument to a lost cause still stands in the middle of their town. Today, if this scene were reenacted, the script must be written quite differently. One or both of the women talk about the statue offends them. They would curse the white establishment for not removing or demolishing the statue. The change in tone and attitude is quite striking but not encouraging. (It would require another essay to explore the importance of maintaining our historical consciousness in order to learn from it.)

The second story comes from another episode of the same program— number 8 in season 5—which tells the story of a successful black man, who had purchased a new Packard automobile in 1948 and who was murdered by a white man for no other reason than he was too successful. The crime is solved forty-three years later by Sweet, now an officer on the local police force and the great-grandson of the murdered victim. The end of the episode, finds Sweet with his boss, Sheriff Bill Gillespie, at the site where the victim had been secretly buried years before in a wooded area, which has now been developed as a public park. White and black children are on the swings, side by side, playing together over the burial site of Sweet's murdered great-grandfather.

Sweet wonders whether they should exhume the body and bury it elsewhere. He reflects about where it now lies, "Couldn't be in a nicer place." Then, after a pause, "I wish he could have seen all this."

He turns to the Sheriff, and asks, "Things are better, aren't they chief? They're not great. But they're better, right?

Chief Gillespie agrees, "Yes, son, they're better, a whole lot better."

When one considers the dark history of Jim Crow and hundreds of extra judicial lynchings, there is little comparison with the situation of blacks in America today. Nevertheless, as Sweet says, "they're not great." Racism has not been eradicated; police brutality is an unfortunate realtiy; and racist judges discriminate against blacks. Nevertheless, the United States has made great strides in treating all of its citizens as they deserve without regard to the color of their skin. However, sadly today a large segment of our society, mostly the elite, finds it politically incorrect to agree with Sweet that, "Things are better."

The third story came to me recently from a granddaughter, whose sister happens to be married to a black man, a change in itself from the sixties that I believe is positive.[15]   Sarah worked her way through college, graduated from nursing school and now works in an ICU cardiac unit of a Cincinnati hospital. Like her siblings, she attended an integrated Christian school where she had both black and white friends. She recently ran into one of these black friends, who found it difficult to celebrate my granddaughter's success. This friend dismissed her success as a consequence merely of her color. She accused her of reaching her professional goal only because she was white and the special privilege her color bestowed upon her.

Her simplistic perspective and summary dismissal of Sarah's success due merely to "white privilege" did nothing to enhance my granddaughter's affection for a black childhood friend. If Sarah had become a nurse in 1970 instead of today, it would have made more sense to attribute it to white privilege. What is striking, however, is that in 1970 I could not have imagined that a black friend would have discounted and disparaged Sarah's achievements.

The focus of blacks I knew in 1970 was not on minimizing the success of whites but upon maximizing their own. Young blacks, who marched and suffered for their rights in the 1960's, strove to have the same opportunities as their white neighbors. The black power movement energized by the slogan "Black is beautiful" sounded like Frederick Douglas, who

---

[15] Indeed, I believe that the final eradication of all forms of racism will depend upon the eradication of color differences in the population due to intermarriage and miscegenation, a point I have made in the chapter, "Sexual Roots of Racism."

explained that what Negroes wanted in the nineteenth century was simply to "be left alone."

These changes have led to an increasing racial divisiveness fed by the advance of identity politics which celebrates the racial, ethnic, and gender identity of designated groups of victims while the rest of us, especially us white, heterosexual males, serve the role of persecutors and oppressors.

If "whiteness" is a reason for shame in those so afflicted, some will inevitably react and embrace their "whiteness" proudly. I might even be tempted to join a proud white parade with the slogan: "We are proud white men with testosterone coursing in our veins." Otherwise, unless I identify as a young, black lesbian, I fear I may endure a long sentence in purgatory to atone for being a decrepit, old, pale, straight male.

Seriously, the nonsense spouted by the prophets of racial identity and the divisiveness it perpetuates is the most regrettable change in race relations I have noted in the twenty-first century.

Signs of Systemic Racism

There is debate over whether America or to what extent America is a racist country and whether racism is baked into our political, economic, and educational structures. Racist comments by white nationalists or the targeting of black motorists by some policemen do demonstrate that racism at the *individual* level is alive and well in our country. However, these are not as such signs of *systemic* racism.

According to progressives, the demolition of Jim Crow by the civil rights legislation of the 60's and the positive changes in education, government, and business practices did not eradicate systemic racism. The evidence for that assertion is based upon the obvious differences that obtain today in the educational and economic achievements between blacks and whites.

Thomas Sowell explains how using differences in achievement serve as *a prior* proof of racial discrimination.

[This] conception of discrimination has a strong hold on many in the media and the academic world today, as well as among political and legal elites. For them, differences in "life chances" define discrimination. If a black child does not have the same likelihood as a white child of growing up to become an executive or a scientist, then there is racial discrimination by this definition, even if the same rules and standards are applied to both in schools, the workplace, and everywhere else. For those with this definition of discrimination, creating "a level playing field" means equalizing probabilities of success. Criteria which operate to prevent this are considered by them to be discriminatory in effect, even if not in intent.[16]

I do not have the expertise to to properly critique this understanding for the evidence of systemic racism. For that I turn to a scholar who has done extensive research on the causes of difference in achievement by different racial and ethnic groups. For those who are open to the evidence that different outcomes cannot prove discrimination I highly recommend that the reader read the entire essay from which the quotation above has been excerpted. However, in one sentence Sowell has reached this: "It would be no feat to fill a book with statistical disparities that have nothing to do with discrimination.[17] What would be a real feat would be to get people to realize that *correlation is not causation* [emphasis added]—especially when the numbers fit their preconceptions.

Going beyond Sowell I suggest that to uncover systemic racism requires a more critical examination of the structure and policies of our public institutions, structures and policies, which

---

[16] "Discrimination, Economics, and Culture" in https://www.hoover.org/sites/default/files/uploads/documents /0817998721_167.pdf

[17] Sowell: "Numerous, documented examples can be found in just two recent books of mine: *Conquests and Cultures* (Basic Books, 1998), pp. 43, 124, 125, 168, 221–222; *Migrations and Cultures* (Basic Books, 1996), pp. 4, 17, 30, 31, 567, 118, 121, 122–123, 126, 130, 135, 152, 154, 157, 158, 162, 164, 167, 176, 177, 179, 182, 193, 196, 201, 211, 212, 213, 215, 224, 226, 251, 258, 264, 265, 275, 277, 278, 289, 290, 297, 298, 300, 305, 306, 310, 313, 314, 318, 320, 323–324, 337, 342, 345, 353–354, 354–355, 355, 356, 358, 363, 366, 372–373. Extending the search for intergroup statistical disparities to the writings of others would of course increase the number of examples exponentially, even when leaving out those cases where discrimination might be a plausible cause of the disparities."

are based on the success of liberals in capturing the media, our educational institutions, the board rooms of our major corporations, and entrenched government bureaucracies. Ironically, compared to the self-righteous rhetoric of liberals who regularly hurl racist epithets against their conservative neighbors, it appears that most signs of systemic racism are rooted in liberal assumptions about race and how racial differences should be addressed in all of our major institutions. For example:

- Race conscious policies of schools, universities, and corporations imply an assumption of the intellectual inferiority of blacks and their inability to complete with other races.

- High tax, low growth economic polices leave low income blacks the last to be employed and the first to be laid off.

- Resistance to school choice by school unions and their Democratic patrons condemns lower income black families to failing public schools for their children.

- Unlimited abortion policies perpetuate the disproportionate abortions of black babies.

- Progressive public welfare policies encourage economic dependency based on the assumption of poor blacks'—and poor white's—incompetence to care for themselves thereby leaving the dominant, politically elite whites in a controlling, one-up position over their dependent subjects. Sowell again: "Although the big word on the left is 'compassion,' the big agenda on the left is dependency."

Racism has not been eliminated from our institutions. But contrary to the popular notion that the support of systemic racism primarily afflicts those whom elites categorize as "deplorables," who "cling to their guns or religion," we find that a more subtle form of racism drives the liberal policies that treat blacks as if they were simply a darker color of that despised group. Systemic racism is the responsibility of elite progressives, both white and black, not racist whites.

Race and Relationships in Sunshine City
by Joe Smith

Joe Smith is an African-American who proudly served as a police officer for the city of Saint Petersburg for twenty-six years. Afterwards he became the first black to serve as the Assistant Director of the Pinellas County Law Enforcement Academy at Saint Petersburg College. He is active in many community boards and is a member of the Saint Petersburg Midtown Rotary Club.

Noted author James Joyner described himself as, "American by Birth, Southern by the Grace of God." I am an American, a proud Southerner, born and raised in Saint Petersburg, Florida, a wonderful city on the Gulf Coast of Florida. My hometown is known as the "Sunshine City" because on average we enjoy 248 sunny days per year. I am proud to say the Sun is bright and it shines on all without regard to the color of their skin.

St. Petersburg, in my mind, has always been a delightful location for children to grow up. When I was a child, my dad said, "This city is great! Where else in the world can you cast a fishing line to catch fish or pick citrus fruit right from a tree?"

A Color Blind Childhood

The discussion of how we formulate our ideas and thoughts surrounding the conversation of race relations in America is intriguing. We are better served as human once we realize that all of us are part of the human race. As a black man, I have had the gracious and humbling opportunity to serve as a law enforcement professional for over 25 years. While many might believe it is because of privilege or position that I have been able to coast through life, I understand it is because of my unique life experiences, especially the support of those who came before me. These have all shaped me and have affected how I have relate to others and my outlook on race and relationships.

Relationships start with conversation. Conversing with people is nothing new to me. As a product of integrated schools and integrated sports teams, I have been exposed to many different people and engaged in many conversations. I thank my parents for my exposure to many different people. As a child growing up during American Civil Rights Movement, my parents like many other African-American parents, sheltered their children from the worst conflict of that era and gave me an integrated experience. My parents advocated for peaceful resolution to social conflict that were advocated by great national leaders, such as Martin Luther King Jr. and President John F. Kennedy.

I believe my mother and father hoped to create an atmosphere for their children so that we could maintain a child's view of the world. I thank my parents for sheltering me from the more cynical perspectives that strained race relations in this country. I believe racist behavior is a behavior learned through observations of others. I am thankful that I came into the world during a time when our country identified the problem of racism.

My third-grade teacher, Mr. Thornton, was a white man brought into an African-American school to integrate the staff and the school. I remember Mr. Thornton as a kind gentleman with a great sense of humor. He always smiled and laughed at life.

I also remember that Mr. Thornton wore clothes that did not match in color. Mr. Thornton often came to school wearing a blue shirt, brown pants, red socks, and brown shoes. I did not think it was a big deal how he dressed. After all, I was a third-grade boy that only owned one pair of school shoes. However, many of the more fashionably conscious third grade girls would always tell Mr. Thornton, "Your clothes don't match." Mr. Thornton would simply laugh and say, "I am color blind." He explained how this prevented him from accurately distinguishing different colors. He said, "I see everything as gray."

As an intelligent third grader, I assumed Mr. Thornton also saw people in shades of gray. I have not seen Mr. Thornton since the third grade, but he impressed upon me that I should not see people as colored one way or another, but that I should see people as people, a simple but important lesson to teach a third grader. As an adult, I have wondered if Mr. Thornton was color blind at all. Thank you, Mr. Thornton.

Life's lessons chip away at us and mold us into the person we are. The person I am today has been molded by my personal journey. The experience of being the first African-American quarterback at a predominately (87%) white school is one I particularly remember. One might suppose that it was a huge challenge. However, this experience was not an emotional challenge because it was my life. I had nothing to compare the experience of being the first of a race to have an opportunity of establishing a positive course of history. I do remember that I was surrounded with wonderful teammates, who understood how to win on and off the field. I know each teammate displayed acceptance of me as a person and I am grateful for their friendship and he fellowship we enjoyed including the prayer that was a part of our weekly Friday night pre-game activity. (You know, the team that prays together.)

I say "thank you" to others, especially my high school coach, Bob Stephens, and my mother. I'll always remember their boundless and unwavering support. She was a strong African-American woman, and he was a wonderful white man, who formed a relationship with me that transcended race and turned a teenager into a man.

I am also proud of the relationship with my high school football team and what we accomplished. Our winning football program changed the trajectory of a football program that had previously never had a winning season. Despite racial differences and growing up in turbulent times, we created relationships and bonds that remain intact today. We remain lifelong friends, and I feel that to this day we respect each other as people regardless of the color of our skin.

After college, I had the opportunity to become an assistant coach for eight years of the varsity team at my high school alma maters. We not only continued to build a winning tradition but also had an even bigger responsibility of building character in young men. The significance of life and the meaning of human equality, which Mr. Thornton taught and instilled in me years earlier was passed on to the many young men I coached.

Race, Relationships and Faith

I would be remiss if I didn't mention my church. It can be a challenge to follow the religious teaching, which admonishes us to love one another and to understand why the church should be racially segregated. When we Christians don't embrace the opportunity to communicate with each other, it is difficult for all of us to love one another as God loves us. It has been said that when you are living a life, you are not able to see anything that is special or unusual because it is your life! When you are doing what God teaches us through Scripture to love one another, you might assume everyone is living a righteous life of loving and helping others.

I have been told that my church is unique and that we should highlight our uniqueness. We are racially quite diverse, 50% percent white and 50% percent people of color. Our church is diverse in other ways. We have the grace to ignore the borders of the world around us. We celebrate members from different regions of the country and from other countries around the world. At Lakeview Presbyterian Church we have united to confess the biblical teaching of our Lord by spreading the message of love.

I am proud that my church has a history of being socially conscious and getting involved in issues that impact other people. The congregation played a role in raising awareness of the conditions of the workers during the sanitation strike of the

1960's. We also participated in our community's debates regarding affordable housing debate and education disparities in our schools in the 1970's.

We have also been involved in addressing the problem of food deserts in which under-served communities do not have available a nearby a market with fresh, healthy foods. For example, my church has been the community leader in a very popular food and clothing bank, Operation Attack (OA). Operation Attack was born November 1967, as the brainchild of the late Dr. Edward L. Cole Jr. At that time Dr. Cole was a Presbyterian ruling elder, a city council member and a pediatrician who was concerned about families in need. Later, Dr. Cole became mayor of St. Petersburg. Dr. Cole's use Operation Attack to attack one of the problems addressed by the War on Poverty.

Dr. Cole asked Lakeview Presbyterian for an initial contribution of $900. The church session voted to make it a part of its mission work in the community and continued to support this mission for over 50 years. Eventually other Presbyterian churches joined the project. Word spread to other denominations and into the community, and others joined in. Today 15 churches support OA.

The reason I mention the ministry of my church is not to beat our chest but to point out what can be done to humbly help others! We are all servants of God trying our best to help people!

Human Relations

Since becoming an adult, I have referred to St. Petersburg as the most liberal conservative city I have seen. We have lived through civil unrest, a history of conversations on inequalities in our educational system, and public concerns about police bias. These issues date back to a time before my birth, but their impact sadly endures to this day even if we assume that most people strive for fairness to all.

I have had the privilege of working as a law enforcement officer, yes, a police officer, for more than two decades. The honorable law enforcement profession has been constructively challenged on its fundamental concept of fairness and justice. An honorable police profession must be focused on serving people in order to make a constructive difference within a community.

Serving as a police officer in a community, in which I was raised, is a tremendous honor and an opportunity to assist people facing life's challenges. I served people that I grew up with, people I knew, and thus, people with whom I could relate. I always understood that my effectiveness as a police officer was based upon my relationship with the community. Serving my own hometown has been an opportunity to protect and serve my community. Many other police officers and law enforcement agencies also work to create a positive relationship with their community. I have always prided myself on being a part of this tradition based upon an understanding that we must work together to resolve problems in our community. If one understands his position as a humble servant of the people, it is easy for a law enforcement professional to be inclusive.

Taking a Stand for Justice

Effective police community relations has been a subject for discussion all of my life. As a college student in 1981 at Florida A&M University, I marched to our state capital in Tallahassee after Arthur Mc Duffie died in custody of the police. This peaceful demonstration was my first opportunity to be involved in this important issue. One purpose of college is to encourage people to be aware of the concerns of the world and to contribute to their positive resolution.

McDuffie was a successful African-American man who had served our country as a Marine. After his military service, he became a successful insurance agent. One Sunday afternoon McDuffie riding his motorcycle ride when he became involved in a high-speed police chase and was killed at the hands of five police officers. I remember walking to the capital and seeing a sea of people as on the road we had traveled. I had never seen so many people of color. After all, at that time minorities comprised only twelve to thirteen percent of Florida's population.

I do not remember the name of the man that spoke to those who had assembled at the steps of the capital, but I do remember what he said. He stated that in the 1950's he had marched on the capital, and he recounted the story of the death of an African-American male had been killed then while in police custody. He then stated he had also marched in the 1960's to protest the death of another African-American male who also died while in police custody. He the again then stated that he had marched in the 1970's and when another African-American male had died while in police custody.

At the protest demonstration the speaker's voice cracked with emotion as he told us that he stood once again on the steps of the Florida State Capital Building asking for an end to police killing innocent men of color and for the police who are involved to be brought to justice. His speech brought home to me the painful reality of how police without warrant can and do kill African-American men. The issue was clearly defined, and I felt that surely all of the people in attendance that day could move the needle toward justice. I was sadly mistaken. Since 1981 many other people of color have inexplicably died while in police custody. Thus, it is necessary to continue to address this issue. Among the changes that must occur, if real equality and justice are ever to be achieved, law enforcement training must be geared to push the needle farther.

A police officer one must develop and maintain with the community the relationship of a humble servant. The police are employed to help people. Their job is simple--to help! I was given this wise counsel by one of the first African-American police officers in the city, Robert Keys. Many of the first African-American officers shared stories of how they created Boy Scout troops, coached little league programs, and helped people find jobs. These officers helped people even when they themselves did not receive justice or respect. An article in the *St. Petersburg Times* carried the following report:

> Freddie Crawford did not always carry his gun when he patrolled the streets of St. Petersburg in the 1960s. "I didn't need it," said Crawford, now 77. "Those people, they knew me. I knew them." Crawford's biggest challenge as an officer was not the people; it was the racist and segregated system in which he worked. At that time, black officers in St. Petersburg couldn't arrest whites, work in certain parts of town or move up the ranks. Things got so bad that in 1965, a dozen of them sued the city for discrimination. They prevailed, and became known as the Courageous 12.

I remember Officer Robert Keys, one of the Courage 12, speaking to me when I was a rookie police officer. I did not think Officer Keys even knew me, but as I walked from the police read-off room, Officer Keys said, "Hey rookie–I don't know if he knew my name–you're doing a great job of arresting people. Just remember, when you get to the end of your career, you want to have some people that you have helped along the way." Officer Keys put a toothpick back into his mouth, turned, and walked away. That advice from Officer Keys shaped my career as a police officer, a law enforcement trainer, and a police academy administrator. As I reflect upon my service as a police officer, I understand that it is an awesome responsibility to work in an environment where people trust you to do the right thing every time. It is the responsibility of us police to understand our commitment and to live up to the challenge of being absolutely trustworthy. As police officers, we are only as good as the service we provide our community.

The 1800's social reformer Theodore Parker has said that, "The arc of the moral universe is long, but it bends towards justice." Nevertheless, I believe that if you wish to change anything, you must do something to create the change. Isaac

Newton's first law states that an object will remain at rest or in uniform motion in a straight line unless compelled to change its state by the action of an external force. I believe people will accept injustice unless we actually take action to promote justice and fairness for everyone.

The individual that acts as a catalyst for change does bend the arc of the moral universe toward truth. I believe the best healer of past injustice is time. Blacks now serve at all levels in law enforcement agencies. Black men lead two of Tampa Bay's biggest police agencies. I am disappointed that it has only been 50 years since that landmark case in which twelve Saint Petersburg Police Officers sued the city for the opportunity to patrol and serve their community like their white colleague. Those 12 officers were hired in a time in which they were not respected as a police officers where they worked, but they persevered to make a difference for greater equality in the next generation.

Our nation is once again grappling with widespread unrest over issues of race and justice.
The Black Lives Matter movement is a continuation of America's history to voice our continuing concerns. Black peoples still fear unjust treatment by a society that has a documented history of unfairness and inhumane treatment of its minority population. As we move toward the future, I remain hopeful, and I believe that we will see fundamental change resulting in respect for all. Nevertheless, positive change will require effort by those who use their power to promote real justice for all of us.

A Simple Philosophy of Life

I live a simple life with the simple philosophy of judging people by the character of their deeds. To accept a person by how they treat others also implies actually talking with people and enjoying conversations that promote building relationships. As a humble law enforcement professional, I have built, as others built in me, a career of color blind relationships and helping people regardless of color. In church I serve with others in a relationship of love regardless of race.

As an African-American boy was born during the 1960's where my parents sheltered me from the racial conflict of that era, I was molded into a man who respects, loves, and cherishes all people. I remember the stories of African-American parents who lived through Jim Crow and protected their children from the worst consequences of racial discrimination of that era. I also remember my mother crying while watching news coverage of the assassination of Dr. Martin Luther King Jr., on April 4, 1968. However, as a child clinging to my mother, I sensed a solemn feeling. It felt like a dark day in the Sunshine City.

Resources

https://www.washingtonpost.com/archive/politics/1980/05/21/mcduffie-death-it-seemed-to-be-open-shut-case/181a3552-c09d-4652-afb1-a9f4f0998a23/?utm_term=.f555310b7d99

http://www.tampabay.com/news/publicsafety/st-petersburgs-courageous-12-officers-see-familiar-struggle-50-years-later/2231715